Fluent Tibetan

Volume Four

VOCABULARY

GRAMMAR

TAPE ERRATA

Contents

Tape Errata   879

VOCABULARY

Three Vocabularies are given: first, in Unit-by-Unit form providing easy access to the words learned to any specific point; then, Tibetan to English in Tibetan alphabetical order; and finally English to Tibetan in English alphabetical order

Unit-by-Unit Vocabulary

UNIT 4

གཟུགས་པོ་	body	སྐུ་གཟུགས་	body (h)
བདེ་པོ་	healthy	ཨ་མེ་རི་ཀ	America/ American
བོད་པ་	Tibetan	ཨིན་ཇི་	English person or Westerner[1]
ང་	I	ང་ཚོ་/ང་རང་ཚོ་	we
ཁྱེད་རང་	you (singular)	ཁྱེད་རང་	you (h singular)
ཁྱེད་རང་ཚོ་/ཁྱེད་ཚོ་	you (plural)	ཁྱེད་རང་ཚོ་	you (h plural)
ཁོ་/ཁོ་རང་	he	ཁོང་	he/she (h)
མོ་/མོ་རང་	she	ཁོང་	she/he (h)
ཁོ་ཚོ་/ཁོ་རང་ཚོ་	they (m)	ཁོང་ཚོ་	they (m/f) (h)
མོ་རང་ཚོ་	they (f)	ཁོང་ཚོ་	they (f/m) (h)

Names

བཀྲ་ཤིས་	good luck/auspicious	བདེ་སྐྱིད་	healthy-happy [used as personal name for female only]
ཚེ་རིང་	long life [life-long]	རྡོ་རྗེ་	thunderbolt [Sanskrit: *vajra*]
སྐལ་བཟང་	good fortune [fortune-good]	སྒྲོལ་མ་	savioress (a goddess) [Sanskrit: Tārā; used as a personal name for female only]
བློ་བཟང་	good mind [mind-good]	སྒྲོལ་དཀར་	White Tārā [Tārā-white; used as a personal name for female only]

---

[1] Another commonly used term is ཕྱི་རྒྱལ་ meaning "foreigner". Still another term is ནུབ་ཕྱོགས་པ་, "person from the West".

བསྟན་འཛིན་	bearer of the teachings [teachings-bearer]	རྒྱ་མཚོ་	ocean [vast-lake]
པད་མ་	lotus [transliteration of the Sanskrit *padma*]	ཉི་མ་	sun [often named so because of being born on Sunday]
དཔལ་ལྡན་	glorious [glory-possessing]	ཟླ་བ་	moon [often named so because of being born on Monday]
དོན་གྲུབ་	accomplished the purpose [purpose-accomplished; Sanskrit: *Siddhārtha*]	རྣམ་རྒྱལ་	conquering
འཇིགས་མེད་	fearless [fear-without; used as a personal name for male only]	འཕྲིན་ལས་	exalted activities
ཐུབ་བསྟན་	teaching of the Muni [Muni-teaching]	ངག་དབང་	power of speech [speech-power]
བསོད་ནམས་	merit		

UNIT 5

རྒྱ་གར་བ་	Indian	ཨུ་རུ་སུ་	Russian
རྒྱ་མི་	Chinese	ཕ་རན་སི་	French
སྙིང་རྗེ་	compassion	ཐུགས་རྗེ་	compassion (h)
ཆེ་	great, big, large	ཐུགས་རྗེ་ཆེ་	thank you
སུ་	who (interrogative pronoun)		

UNIT 6

རྒྱ་ནག་	China	རྒྱ་གར་	India
བོད་	Tibet	ཁ་ཅ་ན་	Canada
ཨིན་ཇིའི་ལུང་པ་	England[1]	འཇར་མན་	Germany

---

[1] Tibetans also say ཨིང་ལན་. This is technically more correct but is less frequently used.

ཕ་རན་སི་	France	འབྲས་ལྗོངས་	Sikkim
འབྲུག་ཡུལ་	Bhutan	རྡོ་རྗེ་གླིང་	Darjeeling
ལ་དྭགས་	Ladakh	ཀ་ཏུ་མན་དུ་	Kathmandu
དིལ་ལི་	Delhi	རྡོ་རྗེ་གདན་	Bodh Gaya
ལྷ་ས་	Hla-ša	སྨན་ཁང་	hospital
སློབ་གྲྭ་/སློབ་གྲྭ་	school	ཟ་ཁང་	restaurant
དགོན་པ་	monastery	ཚོང་ཁང་	store
ནང་	home	གཟིམ་ཁང་	home (h)
འགྲོ་	to go	ཕེབས་	to go, to come (h)
ཁྲོམ་	market	དོ་	let's (mild imperative)
བྱས་ན་	well then (literally, "if done")	ང་གཉིས་	we two, the two of us (literally, "I" and "two")
མཉམ་དུ་	together	ཕྱུན་རྒྱས་	together (h)
ག་པར་	where (interrogative particle)		

UNIT 7

ཁ་ལག་	food	ཞལ་ལག་	food (h)
ཚལ་	vegetable or stir-fry dish	བཞེས་ཚལ་	vegetable or stir-fry dish (h)
འོ་མ་	milk	ཆབ་ལོ་	milk (h)
ཆུ་	water	ཆབ་	water (h)
ཤ་	meat	གསོལ་ཀུ་མ་	meat (h)
འབྲས་	rice	བཞེས་འབྲས་	rice (h)
བག་ལེབ་	bread	བཞེས་བག་	bread (h)
ཇ་	tea	གསོལ་ཇ་	tea (h)

ཞོ་	yogurt	གསོལ་ཞོ་	yogurt (h)
ཆང་	beer, barley wine	མཆོད་ཆང་	beer, barley wine (h)
ཚ་ལུ་མ་	orange	བཞེས་ལུ་མ་	orange (h)
ཨམ་	mango	ཀེ་ལ་	banana
སྣུམ་	oil	བཞེས་སྣུམ་	oil (h)
ཤིང་ཏོག་	fruit	པད་ཚལ་	cabbage
ཀུ་ཤུ་	apple	བཞེས་ཤུ་	apple (h)
སྐྱོང་ལ་ཕུག་	carrot	རྒུན་འབྲུམ་	grape
ཞོག་ཁོག་	potato	བཞེས་ཞོག་	potato (h)
ཙོང་	onion	བཞེས་ཙོང་	onion (h)
ཤོག་བུ་ [1]	paper	ཕྱག་ཤོག་	paper (h)
དེབ་	book	ཕྱག་དེབ་	book (h)
སྨྱུ་གུ་	pen	ཕྱག་སྨྱུག་	pen (h)
ཚགས་པར་	magazine	ཞ་སྨྱུག་	pencil
ཤིང་ཏོག་ཚོང་མཁན་	fruit seller	བག་ལེབ་ཚོང་མཁན་	baker, bread seller
གློག་བརྙན་ཁང་	movie theater	སྦྲག་ཁང་	post office
ཆང་ཁང་	tavern	ཇ་ཁང་	tea house, tea stall
དཔེ་མཛོད་ཁང་	library		
བཟའ་	to eat	མཆོད་	to eat (h)
འཐུང་	to drink	མཆོད་	to drink (h)
ཀློག་	to read	ལྷགས་ཀློག་གནང་	to read (h)

---

[1] Pronounced s̄hu-gu.

ཉོ་	to buy	གཉེགས་	to buy (h)
ལྡག་	to lick	ལྡག་གནང་	to lick (h)
ཕ་གི་	that over there	ཕ་གིར་	over there, there
ཡ་གི་	that up there	ཡ་གིར་	up there
མ་གི་	that down there	མ་གིར་	down there
དེ་	that	ནང་ལ་	in, inside
འདི་	this	འདིར་	here
ག་རེ་	what (interrogative particle)	དང་	and

UNIT 9

དེ་རིང་	today	སང་ཉིན་	tomorrow
གནངས་ཉིན་ཁ་/ནངས་ཉིན་	day after tomorrow	ཉིན་གུང་	noon
ཡག་པོ་	good	སྡུག་ཆག་	bad, awful
ཆེན་པོ་	large, big, great	ཆུང་ཆུང་	small, little
ཉུང་ཉུང་	few, a little	མང་པོ་	much, many, a lot
ཁ་ཤས་/འགའ་ཤས་	some, several	ཚང་མ་	all
གསར་པ་	new	རྙིང་པ་	old
གསར་པོ་	pretty new	རྙིང་པོ་	pretty old
སྟེང་ལ་	on, on top of	འོག་ལ་	under, beneath, below
འཁྲིས་ལ་	near, beside	ཆུང་རིང་པོ་	far away, in the distance
མདུན་ལ་	in front of	རྒྱབ་ལ་	behind, in back of
དེ་ཚོ་	those	འདི་ཚོ་	these

རི་	mountain	ལམ་ཁ་	road
གྲོང་ཁྱེར་	city, town[1]	ག་དུས་	when (interrogative particle)
གནས་ཚང་	hotel, inn, hostel	མགྲོན་ཁང་	hotel, inn
ལྷ་ཁང་	temple	ཇོ་ཁང་	Cho-khang
བཙོན་ཁང་	prison	དངུལ་ཁང་	bank
ཚོས་མདོག	color	སྔོན་པོ་	blue
སེར་པོ་	yellow	དཀར་པོ་	white
དམར་པོ་	red	ནག་པོ་	black
ལྗང་ཁུ་	green	རྒྱ་སྨུག / སྨུག་པོ་	brown
གཅིག་	one	གཉིས་	two
གསུམ་	three	བཞི་	four
ལྔ་	five	དྲུག་	six

UNIT 10

ཀུབ་ཀྱག་	chair	ཞབས་ཀྱག་	chair (h)
སྒོ་	door	གཟིམ་སྒོ་	door (h)
དཀར་ཡོལ་	cup	ཞལ་དཀར་	cup (h)
ཅོག་ཙེ་	table	གསོལ་ཅོག་	table (h)
སྐེ་ཁུང་	window	གཡག་ཤ / ཆག་ཤ་	yak meat
བྱ་ཤ་	chicken meat	གླང་ཤ་	beef
ལུག་ཤ་	lamb meat	ཕག་ཤ་	pork
ཉ་ཤ་	fish meat	བོད་ཇ་	Tibetan tea

---

[1] "Town" is also གྲོང་ཚོ་.

ཇ་མངར་མོ་	sweet tea	གསོལ་ཇ་མངར་མོ་	sweet tea (h)
རྩམ་པ་	ground parched barley	གསོལ་ཞིབ་	ground parched barley (h)
སྤག་	parched barley dough	གསོ་བ་	parched barley dough (h)
ཆུ་མངར་མོ་	soda, soft drink	ཆབ་མངར་མོ་	soda, soft drink (h)
ཐུག་པ་	noodle soup[1]	བཞེས་ཐུག་	noodle soup (h)
མོག་མོག་	steamed dumpling	བཞེས་མོག་	steamed dumpling (h)
ཀྱིང་མོག་མོག་ / ཀྱིང་མོག་	steamed dumpling with no filling	སྲན་མ་	pea
གོང་	price	ཕྱགས་གོང་	price (h)
གོང་ཁི་པོ་ / ཁི་པོ་	inexpensive	གོང་ཆེན་པོ་	expensive
མི་	person, man	བུད་མེད་ / སྐྱེ་དམན་	woman
བུ་མོ་	girl/daughter	སྲས་མོ་	girl/daughter (h)
བུ་	boy/son	སྲས་	boy/son (h)
ཕྲུ་གུ་[2]	child	ཨ་བ་	child (h)
སྒོར་མོ་	unit of money (dollar, rupee, franc, etc.)	ཕྱུག་པོ་	rich
ཐང་ག་	scroll painting		
སྐྱུར་མོ་	sour	མངར་མོ་	sweet
འདྲ་མི་འདྲ་	various	དྲང་པོ་	honest
སེམས་བཟང་པོ་	kind, good-hearted	འབྲོག་པ་	nomad
གནམ་གཤིས་	weather	བསིལ་པོ་	cool
ཚ་པོ་	hot	གྲང་མོ་	cold

---

[1] The word ཐུག་པ་ can also be used for rice soup and so forth.

[2] Often pronounced b̄u-gu.

ཐག་ཉེ་པོ་	near, close	ཐག་རིང་པོ་	distant, far
ཞེ་དྲག	very	ཞེད་པོ་ཅིག	very, extremely
ཧ་ཅང་	very	དཔེ་	very, exceptionally
དངོས་གནས་	really	ག་ཚོད་/ག་ཚད་	how much, how many
གཡས་	right	གཡོན་	left
གཡས་ངོས་	right side	གཡོན་ངོས་	left side
གཡས་གཡོན་ལ་	on either side of		
བསྡད་	to sit, to stay	བཞུགས་	to sit, to stay (h)
བསྲེག་[1]	to roast	བསྲེག་གནང་	to roast (h)
རླངས་བཙོས་བརྒྱབ་	to steam	རླངས་བཙོས་བསྐྱོན་	to steam (h)
བརྔོ་	to fry (foods), to parch (barley)	བརྔོས་གནང་	to fry (foods), to parch (barley) (h)
བཟོ་	to make, to prepare	བཟོས་གནང་	to make, prepare (h)
ཚོང་	to sell	ཚོང་བསྐྱོན་	to sell (h)

UNIT 11

གསོལ་ཚིགས་	food (h)	གྲོ་ཞིབ་	flour
མར་	butter	གསོལ་མར་	butter (h)
ཞིམ་པོ་	tasty, delicious	སྦྲོ་པོ་	tasty, delicious (h)
སྐྱིད་པོ་	pleasant, comfortable	སྦྲོ་པོ་	pleasant, comfortable (h)
ཨེ་གེ་	letter	ཕྱག་བྲིས་	letter (h)
དཔེ་ཆ་	Buddhist text (Tibetan style)	ཕྱག་དཔེ་	Buddhist text (Tibetan style, h)
རྡ་རམ་ས་ལ་	Dharamsala	གཞིས་ཀ་རྩེ་	<u>Sh</u>i-ḡa-d̄zé

[1] In Central Tibetan dialect, pronounced d̠a'.

དག་དག་	just right	རིང་པོ་	long
ཐུང་ཐུང་	short	རིང་ཐུང་	length
ཆེན་པོ་	large, great	ཆུང་ཆུང་	little
ཆེ་ཆུང་	size		
ཉེས་པོ་	bad	ཡག་ཉེས་	quality (literally, "good-bad")
གསར་ཤོག་	newspaper	ས་གདན་	rug
སྦུ་པོ་	weak (with beverages)	གར་པོ་	strong (with beverages)
ཚྭ་	salt	ཕྱགས་ཚྭ་	salt (h)
ཕྱེ་མ་ཀ་ར་	sugar	སྐྲ་ཁང་	barber shop
ཨ་མ་ལགས་	mother (h)	པ་ལགས་	father (h)
ཕ་མ་	parents	ཨ་ཅག་ལགས་	sister (h)
བཟའ་ཟླ་	spouse	སྐུ་ཟླ་	spouse (h)
ཁྱི་	dog	ཞི་མི་	cat
དགེ་རྒན་	teacher	སློབ་གྲྭ་བ་	student
དམག་མི་	soldier	མེ་མདའ་	gun
དགོང་དག་	evening	དགོང་དྲོ་	evening
སང་དགོང་	tomorrow evening, next evening	དུས་སང་	next year
གཟའ་ཉི་མ་	Sunday	གཟའ་ཟླ་བ་	Monday
གཟའ་མིག་དམར་	Tuesday	གཟའ་ལྷག་པ་	Wednesday
གཟའ་ཕུར་བུ་	Thursday	གཟའ་པ་སངས་	Friday
གཟའ་སྤེན་པ་	Saturday	ཚེས་པ་	date
བདུན་ཕྲག་	week	གཟའ་འཁོར་	week

ཟླ་བ་	month	ལོ་	year
བྱེད་	to do	གནང་	to do (h)
སློབ་སྦྱོང་བྱེད་	to study	སློབ་སྦྱོང་གནང་	to study (h)
ཡོང་	to come	ཕར་ཚུར་	here and there, there and back
ཕར་	over there	ཚུར་	over here
བསླེབ་	to arrive		
འབྱོར་	to arrive	འབྱོར་གནང་/ ཕེབས་ འབྱོར་གནང་	to arrive (h)
བྲི་	to write, to paint, to draw	བྲིས་གནང་	to write, to paint, to draw (h)
བལྟ་	to look at, to watch	གཟིགས་	to look at, to watch (h)

UNIT 12

བླ་མ་	lama	བཞུ་མར་	lamp
གནམ་གྲུ་	airplane	གནམ་གྲུ་ཐང་	airport
མེ་ཏོག་	flower	མཚོ་	lake
ཁ་པར་	telephone	ཞལ་པར་	telephone (h)
ཁ་པར་བཏང་	to telephone	ཞལ་པར་བཏང་གནང་	to telephone (h)
ལྷགས་པ་/ རླུང་	wind	ལྷགས་པ་རྒྱབ་	to be windy
ཆར་པ་	rain	ཆར་པ་བཏང་	to rain
སྤར་	to ignite, to turn on	སྤར་གནང་	to ignite, to turn on (h)
བསད་	to kill, to turn off	བསད་གནང་	to kill, to turn off (h)
མོ་ཊར་	car	མོ་ཊར་བཏང་	to drive a car
རྨི་ལམ་/ གཉིད་ལམ་	dream		

ཀྲི་ལམ་བཏང་ / གཉིད་ ལམ་བཏང་	to dream	ཀྲི་ལམ་བཏང་གནང་ / གཉིད་ལམ་བཏང་ གནང་	to dream (h)
བོད་སྐད་	Tibetan language	ཨིན་ཇིའི་སྐད་	English language
ཕ་རན་སིའི་སྐད་	French language	རྒྱ་སྐད་	Chinese language
འདི་འདྲ་ / འདི་འདྲས་	in this way, such (literally, "this-like")		
སྐད་ཆ་	conversation	བཀའ་མོལ་	conversation (h)
སྐད་ཆ་བཤད་	to make conversation	བཀའ་མོལ་གསུང་	to make conversation (h)
ལས་ཀ་	work	ཕྱག་ལས་	work (h)
ལས་ཀ་བྱེད་	to work	ཕྱག་ལས་གནང་	to work (h)
རྒྱབ་	to build, to make	སྐྱོན་	to build, to make (h)
སློབ་སྦྱོང་	studies	ངལ་གསོ་	rest
ངལ་གསོ་རྒྱབ་	to rest	ངལ་གསོ་སྐྱོན་	to rest (h)
བསླབ་	to study, to learn	བསླབ་གནང་	to study, to learn (h)
གཡར་	to borrow, to lend	གཡར་གནང་	to borrow, to lend (h)
ཤེས་	to know	མཁྱེན་	to know (h)
མཐོང་	to see	གཟིགས་	to see (h)
ཐུག་	to meet	མཇལ་	to meet (h)
ངོ་ཤེས་	to know someone	ངོ་མཁྱེན་	to know someone (h)
བསམ་	to think	དགོངས་	to think (h)
དགོས་	to need, to want	དགོས་གནང་	to need, to want (h)
མཐུན་	to agree	འགྲིག་	to be correct, to be okay
དྲན་	to remember	དྲན་གནང་	to remember (h)

འཁྱག་	to feel cold	སྐུ་བསིལ་	to feel cold (h)
ན་	to be sick	སྣུང་	to be sick (h)
ཆམས་པ་རྒྱབ་	to catch cold	ཆམས་པ་སྐྱོན་	to catch cold (h)
གོ་	to hear, to understand	གསན་	to hear (h)
ཧ་གོ་	to understand	མཁྱེན་	to understand (h)
ལེན་	to take	བཞེས་	to take, to partake (h)

UNIT 13

ཆུ་ཚོད་	hour, o'clock, watch, clock	དང་ཕྱེད་ཀ་	and a half
སྐར་མ་	minute	ཟིན་པ་	reaching (before the hour)
ད་གིན་	a short time ago	དོ་དགོང་	tonight
གཞེས་ཉིན་ཁ་	two days after tomorrow	གཉིད་འཁུག་	to sleep
སྔ་པོ་	early	ཕྱི་པོ་	late
ན྄་ཉིན་ / ན་ཉིན་	last year	གཞེས་ཉིན་	two years ago
གུང་སེང་	vacation	དང་པོ་	first
དབུས་སྐད་	Central Tibetan dialect	ཁམས་སྐད་	Kham dialect
གཙང་སྐད་	Ḏzang dialect	ལྷ་སའི་སྐད་	Hla-ša dialect
ལས་སླ་པོ་	easy	ཁག་པོ་	difficult
ལྗིད་པོ་	heavy	ཡང་པོ་	light
ཚར་	to finish	གྲུབ་	to finish (h)
བསྡོམ་	to combine, to add	འཐེན་	to reduce, to subtract
བགོ་	to divide, to share	འགོར་	to take time
ཆེ་ཆུང་	size	བདེ་སྡུག་	feeling, comfort

ཚ་གྲང་	temperature	ལྗིད་ཚིད་	weight
མང་ཉུང་	quantity	ཁ་ཆེ་	Muslim
ནང་པ་	Buddhist	ཡེ་ཤུ་པ་	Christian
སོག་པོ་	Mongolian	རིན་པོ་ཆེ་	Rînboché (literally, "precious one"; an epithet for a lama)
གྲྭ་པ་	monk	གྲྭ་ཚང་	monastic college
ཨ་ནེ་	Nun	ཨ་ནེའི་དགོན་པ་	nunnery

UNIT 14

ཁ་བཏགས་	presentation scarf	ས་ཆ་	area, place
ག་ནས་	from where (interrogative particle)	རུ་ལ་	to (someone), at
སྒོ་ང་	egg	བཞེས་སྒོང་	egg (h)
ཟླ་བ་	moon	ཆམ་ཆམ་	stroll, walk
གྲོགས་མོ་	friend (female)	གྲོགས་པོ་	friend (male)
མིང་	name	མཚན་	name (h)
སྐོར་	about	རུ་ནས་	from (someone)
དེ་ནས་	then	ཡང་སྐྱར་	again
གཞུག་ལ་	after	རྗེས་ལ་	after
མདང་ས་དགོང་	last night		
ཁ་ས་	yesterday	ཁ་སིང་	some time ago
སྔོན་ལ་	ago, earlier, previously	སྔོན་མ་	previously
དགའ་པོ་བྱུང་	to enjoy, to like, to feel happy	མཉེས་པོ་བྱུང་	to enjoy, to like, to feel happy (h)
སྦྱང་	to practice, to train, to learn	སྦྱངས་གནང་	to practice, to train, to learn (h)

ཁྱེར་	to bring, to carry	བསྐྱལ་	to bring, to carry (h)
བླུགས་	to pour	བླུགས་གནང་	to pour (h)
སྤྲད་	to give	གནང་	to give, to do (h)
བསྟེར་	to give	གནང་	to give, to do (h)
འཛུལ་	to enter	འཛུལ་གནང་	to enter (h)
ཕྲད་	to meet	མཇལ་ / མཇལ་གནང་	to meet (h)
སྐད་ཆ་དྲིས་	to ask	བཀའ་འདྲི་གནང་	to ask (h)
ཞུས་	to request, to partake	ཞུས་གནང་	to request, to partake (h)
ཕུལ་	to offer	ཕུལ་གནང་	to offer (h)

Tibetan-English Vocabulary

ཀ་

གཏུ་མན་ཏུ་	Kathmandu
ཀུ་ཤུ་	apple
ཀེ་ལ་	banana
ཀྱིང་མོག་མོག་ / ཀྱིང་མོག་	steamed dumpling with no filling
དཀར་པོ་	white
དཀར་ཡོལ་	cup
བཀའ་མོལ་	conversation (h)
བཀའ་འདྲི་གནང་ / བཀའ་འདྲི་གནང་ / བཀའ་འདྲི་གནང་	to ask (h)
བཀྲ་ཤིས་	good luck/auspicious, p.n.
བཀླག་ / ཀློག་ / བཀླགས་	to read
ཀུབ་ཀྱག་	chair
སྐད་ཆ་	conversation
སྐད་ཆ་འདྲི་ / སྐད་ཆ་དྲི་ / སྐད་ཆ་དྲིས་	to ask
སྐར་མ་	minute
སྐལ་བཟང་	good fortune [fortune-good], p.n.
སྐུ་ཁང་	barber shop
སྐུ་ཟླ་	spouse (h)
སྐུ་གཟུགས་	body (h)

སྐུ་བསིལ་ / སྐུ་བསིལ་ / སྐུ་བསིལ་	to feel cold (h)
སྐོར་	about
སྐྱིད་པོ་	pleasant, comfortable
སྐྱུར་མོ་	sour
བསྐྲུན་ / སྐྲུན་ / བསྐྲུནད་	to build, to make, to put (h)

ཁ་

ཁ་ཆེ་	Muslim
ཁ་བཏགས་	presentation scarf
ཁ་ཎ་ཌ་	Canada
ཁ་པར་	telephone
ཁ་པར་གཏང་ / ཁ་པར་གཏོང་ / ཁ་པར་བཏང་	to telephone
ཁ་ལག་	food
ཁ་ཤས་ / འགའ་ཤས་	some, several
ཁ་ས་	yesterday
ཁ་སེང་	some time ago
ཁག་པོ་	difficult
ཁམས་སྐད་	Kham dialect
ཁོ་ / ཁོ་རང་	he
ཁོ་ཚོ་ / ཁོ་རང་ཚོ་	they (m)
ཁོང་	she/he (h)

ཁོང་ཚོ་	they (f/m) (h)	གྲྭ་ཚང་	monastic college
ཁྱི་	dog	གྲང་མོ་	cold
ཁྱེད་རང་	you (h singular)	གྲོ་ཞིབ་	flour
ཁྱོད་རང་	you (singular)	གྲོགས་པོ་	friend (male)
ཁྱེད་རང་ཚོ་	you (h plural)	གྲོགས་མོ་	friend (female)
ཁྱོད་རང་ཚོ་ / ཁྱོད་ཚོ་	you (plural)	གྲོང་ཁྱེར་	city, town
ཁྱེར་ / འཁྱེར་ / ཁྱེར་ད་	to bring, to carry	གླང་ཤ་	beef
ཁྲོམ་	market	གློག་བརྙན་ཁང་	movie theater
མཁྱེན་ / མཁྱེན་ / མཁྱེན་ད་	to know (h)	དགེ་རྒན་	teacher
མཁྱེན་ / མཁྱེན་ / མཁྱེན་ད་	to understand (h)	དགོང་དག / དགོང་དྲོ་	evening
འཁྱག / འཁྱག / འཁྱགས་	to feel cold	དགོངས་ / དགོངས་ / དགོངས་	to think (h)
འཁྲིས་ལ་	near, beside		
		དགོན་པ་	monastery
# ག་		དགོས་ / དགོས་ / དགོས་	to need, to want
ག་དུས་	when (interrogative particle)	དགོས་གནང་ / དགོས་ གནང་ / དགོས་གནང་	to need, to want (h)
ག་ནས་	from where (interrogative particle)	བགོ་ / བགོ་ / བགོས་	to divide, to share
ག་པར་	where (interrogative particle)	མགྲོན་ཁང་	hotel, inn
ག་ཚོད་ / ག་ཚད་	how much, how many	འགྲིག / འགྲིག / འགྲིགས་	to be correct, to be okay
ག་རེ་	what (interrogative particle)	འགྲུབ་ / འགྲུབ་ / གྲུབ་	to finish (h)
གར་པོ་	strong (with beverages)	འགྲོ་ / འགྲོ་ / ཕྱིན་	to go
གུང་སེང་	vacation	རྒུན་འབྲུམ་	grape
གོ་ / གོ་ / གོ་	to hear, to understand	རྒྱ་སྐད་	Chinese language
གོང་	price	རྒྱ་གར་	India
གོང་ཁི་པོ་ / ཁི་པོ་	inexpensive	རྒྱ་གར་བ་	Indian
གོང་ཆེན་པོ་	expensive	རྒྱ་ནག	China
གྲྭ་པ་	monk	རྒྱ་མི་	Chinese

རྒྱ་སྨུག / སྨུག་པོ་	brown	ངལ་གསོ་བརྒྱབ / ངལ་གསོ་རྒྱབ / ངལ་གསོ་བརྒྱབས་	to rest
རྒྱ་མཚོ་	ocean [vast-lake], p.n.		
རྒྱང་རིང་པོ་	far away, in the distance	ངོ་མཐྲིན / ངོ་མཐྲིན / ངོ་མཐྲིད་	to know someone (h)
རྒྱབ་ལ་	behind, in back of		
སྒང་ལ་	on, on top of	ངོ་ཤེས / ངོ་ཤེས / ངོ་ཤེས་	to know someone
སྒེ་ཁུང་	window		
སྒོ་	door	དངུལ་ཁང་	bank
སྒོང་	egg	དངོས་གནས་	really
སྒོང་ལ་ཕུག	carrot	མངར་མོ་	sweet
སྒོར་མོ་	unit of money (dollar, rupee, franc, etc.)	ལྔ་	five
སྒྲོལ་དཀར་	White Tārā ["Tārā-white"; used as a personal name for female only]	སྔ་པོ་	early
		སྔོན་པོ་	blue
སྒྲོལ་མ་	savioress (a goddess) [Sanskrit: Tārā; used as p.n. for female only]	སྔོན་མ་	previously
		སྔོན་ལ་	ago, earlier, previously
བརྒྱབ / རྒྱབ / བརྒྱབས་	to build, to make, to put	བངོ་ / ངོ་ / བངོས་	to fry (foods), to parch (barley)
ང་		བངོས་གནང་ / བངོས་གནང་ / བངོས་གནང་	to fry (foods), to parch (barley) (h)
ང་	I		
ང་གཉིས་	we two, the two of us (lit., "I" and "two")	**ཙ་**	
ང་ཚོ་ / ང་རང་ཚོ་	we	ཙོག་ཙེ་	table
ངག་དབང་	power of speech [speech-power], p.n.	གཅིག	one
ངལ་གསོ་	rest	**ཆ་**	
ངལ་གསོ་བསྐྱོན / ངལ་གསོ་སྐྱོན / ངལ་གསོ་བསྐྱོད་	to rest (h)	ཆང་	beer, barley wine
		ཆང་ཁང་	tavern
		ཆབ་	water (h)
		ཆབ་མངར་མོ་	soda, soft drink (h)
		ཆབ་ཞོ་	milk (h)

ཆམ་ཆམ་	stroll, walk
ཆམས་པ་བསྐྱོན་ / ཆམས་པ་སྐྱོན་ / ཆམས་པ་བསྐྱོནད་	to catch cold (h)
ཆམས་པ་བཀྱབ་ / ཆམས་པ་ཀྱབ་ / ཆམས་པ་བཀྱབས་	to catch cold
ཆར་པ་	rain
ཆར་པ་གཏང་ / ཆར་པ་གཏོང་ / ཆར་པ་བཏང་	to rain
ཆུ་	water
ཆུ་མངར་མོ་	soda, soft drink
ཆུ་ཚོད་	hour, o'clock, watch, clock
ཆུང་ཆུང་	little, small
ཆེ་ / ཆེན་པོ་	big, large, great
ཆེ་ཆུང་	size (lit., "big-small")
ཆེན་པོ་	large, big, great
མཆོད་ / མཆོད་ / མཆོད་	to drink (h)
མཆོད་ / མཆོད་ / མཆོད་	to eat (h)
མཆོད་ཆང་	beer, barley wine (h)

ཇ་

ཇ་	tea
ཇ་ཁང་	tea house, tea stall
ཇ་མངར་མོ་	sweet tea
ཇོ་ཁང་	<u>C</u>ho-khang
མཇལ་ / མཇལ་ / མཇལད་	

མཇལ་གནང་ / མཇལ་གནང་ / མཇལ་གནང་	to meet (h)
འཇར་མན་	Germany
འཇིགས་མེད་	fearless [fear-without; used as p.n. for male only]
ལྷགས་ཀློག་གནང་ / ལྷགས་ཀློག་གནང་ / ལྷགས་ཀློག་གནང་	to read (h)
ལྷགས་གོང་	price (h)
ལྷགས་ཚྭ་	salt (h)
ལྗང་ཁུ་	green
ལྗིད་པོ་	heavy

ཉ་

ཉ་ཤ་	fish meat
ཉི་མ་	sun, p.n.
ཉིན་གུང་	noon
ཉུང་ཉུང་	few, a little
ཉེས་པོ་	bad
ཉོ་ / ཉོ་ / ཉོས་	to buy
གཉིད་འཁབ་ / གཉིད་འཁགས་ / གཉིད་ཁགས་	to sleep
གཉིས་	two
མཉམ་དུ་	together
རྙིང་པ་	old
རྙིང་པོ་	pretty old
སྙིང་རྗེ་	compassion
བསྙུང་ / སྙུང་ / བསྙུངས་	to be sick (h)

ཏ་

ཏག་ཏག	just right
ཏོ་	let's (mild imperative)
བཏུང་ / འཐུང་ / བཏུངས་	to drink
བསྟན་འཛིན་	bearer of the teachings [teachings-bearer], p.n.
བསྟེར་ / སྟེར་ / བསྟེརད་	to give

ཐ་

ཐག་ཉེ་པོ་	near, close
ཐག་རིང་པོ་	distant, far
ཐང་ག	scroll painting
ཐུག / ཐུག / ཐུག	to meet
ཐུག་པ་	noodle soup
ཐུགས་རྗེ་	compassion (h)
ཐུགས་རྗེ་ཆེ་	thank you
ཐུང་ཐུང་	short
ཐུབ་བསྟན་	teaching of the Muni [Muni-teaching], p.n.
ཐེན་ / འཐེན་ / ཐེནད་	to reduce, to subtract
མཐུན་ / མཐུན་ / མཐུནད་	to agree
མཐུན་གནང་ / མཐུན་ གནང་ / མཐུན་གནང་	to agree (h)
མཐོང་ / མཐོང་ / མཐོང་	to see

ད་

ད་གིན་	short time ago, a
དང་	and
དང་པོ་	first

དང་ཕྱེད་ག	and a half
དུས་སང་	next year
དེ་	that
དེ་ནས་	then
དེ་ཚོ་	those
དེ་རིང་	today
དེབ་	book
དོ་དགོང་	tonight
དོན་གྲུབ་	accomplished the pur- pose [purpose- accomplished; Sanskrit: *Siddhārtha*], p.n.
དྲང་པོ་	honest
དྲན་ / དྲན་ / དྲནད་	to remember
དྲན་གནང་ / དྲན་གནང་ / དྲནད་གནང་	to remember (h)
དྲུག	six
བདུན་ཕྲག	week
བདེ་སྐྱིད་	healthy-happy [used as p.n. for female only]
བདེ་པོ་	healthy
བདེ་ཐུག	feeling, comfort
མདངས་དགོང་	last night
མདུན་ལ་	in front of
འདི་	this
འདི་འདྲ་ / འདི་འདྲས་	in this way, such (lit., "this-like")
འདི་ཚོ་	these
འདིར་	here
འདྲ་མི་འདྲ་	various

རྡོ་རྗེ་	thunderbolt [Sanskrit: *vajra*], p.n.	པད་མ་	lotus [transliteration of Sanskrit *padma*], p.n.
རྡོ་རྗེ་གླིང་	Darjeeling	པད་ཚལ་	cabbage
རྡོ་རྗེ་གདན་	Bodh Gaya	དཔལ་ལྡན་	glorious [glory-possessing], p.n.
སྡུག་ཆག་	bad, awful	དཔེ་	very, exceptionally
བསྡད་ / སྡོད་ / བསྡད་	to sit, to stay	དཔེ་ཆ་	Buddhist text (Tibetan style)
བསྡོམ་ / སྡོམ་ / བསྡོམས་	to combine, to add	དཔེ་མཛོད་ཁང་	library
རྡ་རམ་ས་ལ་	Dharamsala	སྤག་	parched barley dough
སྡེ་ལི་	Delhi	སྤར་ / སྤོར་ / སྤར་ད་	to ignite, to turn on
ན་		སྤར་གནང་ / སྤར་གནང་ / སྤར་གནང་	to ignite, to turn on (h)
ན་ / ན་ / ན་	to be sick		
ནག་པོ་	black	སྤྲད་ / སྤྲོད་ / སྤྲད་	to give
ནང་	home	སྤྲོ་པོ་	pleasant, comfortable (h)
ནང་པ་	Buddhist	ཞིམ་པོ་	tasty, delicious (h)
ནང་ལ་	in, inside	**པ་**	
གནང་ / གནང་ / གནང་	to give, to do (h)	ཕ་གི་	that over there
གནངས་ཉིན་ཁ་ / ནངས་ཉིན་	day after tomorrow	ཕ་གིར་	over there, there
གནམ་གྲུ་	airplane	ཕ་མ་	parents
གནམ་གྲུ་ཐང་	airport	ཕ་རན་སི་	France, French
གནམ་གཤིས་	weather	ཕ་རན་སིའི་སྐད་	French language
གནས་ཚང་	hotel, inn, hostel	ཕག་ཤ་	pork
རྣམ་རྒྱལ་	conquering, p.n.	ཕར་	over there
སྣམས་ / སྣོམ་ / བསྣམས་	to bring, to carry (h)	ཕར་ཚུར་	here and there, there and back
སྣུམ་	oil	ཕུལ་གནང་ / ཕུལ་གནང་ / ཕུལ་གནང་	to offer (h)
པ་			
པུ་ལགས་	father (h)	ཕེབས་ / ཕེབས་ / ཕེབས་	to go, to come (h)

ཕེབས་འབྱོར་གནང་། ཕེབས་འབྱོར་གནང་། ཕེབས་འབྱོར་གནང་	to arrive (h)
ཕྱག་དེབ་	book (h)
ཕྱག་དཔེ་	Buddhist text (Tibetan style, h)
ཕྱག་བྲིས་	letter (h)
ཕྱག་སྨྱུག་	pen (h)
ཕྱག་ལས་	work (h)
ཕྱག་ལས་གནང་། ཕྱག་ལས་གནང་། ཕྱག་ལས་གནང་	to work (h)
ཕྱག་ཤོག་	paper (h)
ཕྱི་པོ་	late
ཕྱུག་པོ་	rich
ཕྲུ་གུ་[1]	child
འཕྲིན་ལས་	exalted activities

བ་

བག་ལེབ་	bread
བག་ལེབ་ཚོང་མཁན་	baker, bread seller
བུ་	boy/son
བུ་མོ་	girl/daughter
བུད་མེད་ / སྐྱེ་དམན་	woman
བོད་	Tibet
བོད་སྐད་	Tibetan language
བོད་ཇ་	Tibetan tea
བོད་པ་	Tibetan
བྱ་ / བྱེད་ / བྱས་	to do

བྱ་ཤ་	chicken meat
བྱས་ན་	well then (lit., "if done")
བྱེ་མ་ཀ་ར་	sugar
བྲི་ / འབྲི་ / བྲིས་	to write, to paint, to draw
བྲིས་གནང་། བྲིས་གནང་། བྲིས་གནང་	to write, to paint, to draw (h)
བླ་མ་	lama
བླང་ / ལེན་ / བླངས་	
བླུག་ / བླུག་ / བླུགས་	to pour
བླུགས་གནང་། བླུགས་གནང་། བླུགས་གནང་	to pour (h)
བློ་བཟང་	good mind [mind-good], p.n.
དབུས་སྐད་	Central Tibetan dialect
འབུལ་ / འབུལ་ / ཕུལ་	to offer
འབྱོར་ / འབྱོར་ / འབྱོརད་ བསླེབ་ / སླེབ་ / བསླེབས་ འབྱོར་གནང་། འབྱོར་ གནང་། འབྱོར་གནང་	to arrive
འབྲས་	rice
འབྲས་ལྗོངས་	Sikkim
འབྲུག་ཡུལ་	Bhutan
འབྲོག་པ་	nomad
སྦྱང་ / སྦྱོང་ / སྦྱངས་	to practice, to train, to learn
སྦྱངས་གནང་། སྦྱངས་ གནང་། སྦྱངས་གནང་	to practice, to train, to learn (h)
སྦྲག་ཁང་	post office

མ་

མ་གི་	that down there
མ་གིར་	down there
མང་ཉུང་	quantity (lit., "many-few"
མང་པོ་	much, many, a lot
མར་	butter
མི་	person, man
མིང་	name
མེ་ཏོག་	flower
མེ་མདའ་	gun
མོ་ / མོ་རང་	she
མོ་ཊ་	car
མོ་ཊར་གཏང་ / མོ་ཊར་ གཏོང་ / མོ་ཊར་བཏང་	to drive a car
མོ་ཊར་བཏང་གནང་ / མོ་ ཊར་བཏང་གནང་ / མོ་ ཊར་བཏང་གནང་	to drive a car (h)
མོ་རང་ཚོ་	they (f)
མོག་མོག་	steamed dumpling
དམག་མི་	soldier
དམར་པོ་	red
རྨི་ལམ་ / གཉིད་ལམ་	dream
རྨི་ལམ་གཏང་ / རྨི་ལམ་ གཏོང་ / རྨི་ལམ་བཏང་	to dream
རྨི་ལམ་བཏང་གནང་ / རྨི་ ལམ་བཏང་གནང་ / རྨི་ ལམ་བཏང་གནང་	to dream (h)
སྨན་ཁང་	hospital

སྨྱུ་གུ་	pen

ཙ་

ཙོང་	onion
གཙང་སྐད་	Dzang dialect
བཙོང་ / འཚོང་ / བཙོངས་	to sell
བཙོན་ཁང་	prison
རྩ་ནས་	from (someone)
རྩ་ལ་	to (someone), at
རྩམ་པ་	ground parched barley

ཚ་

ཚུ་	salt
ཚ་གྲང་	temperature (lit., "hot-cold")
ཚ་པོ་	hot
ཚ་ལུ་མ་	orange
ཚག་པར་	magazine
ཚང་མ་	all
ཚར་ / ཚར་ / ཚར་ད	to finish
ཚལ་	vegetable or stir-fry dish
ཚུར་	over here
ཚེ་རིང་	long life [life-long], p.n.
ཚེས་པ་	date
ཚོང་བསྐྱིན་ / ཚོང་སྐྱིན་ / ཚོང་བསྐྱིནད	to sell (h)
ཚོང་ཁང་	store
ཚོས་མདོག་	color
མཚན་	name (h)

མཚོ་	lake	བཞུ་མར་	lamp
ཇ་		བཞུགས་ / བཞུགས་ / བཞུགས་	to sit, to stay (h)
འཇལ་ / འཇལ་ / འཇལ་	to enter	བཞེས་ / བཞེས་ / བཞེས་	to take, to partake (h)
འཇལ་གནང་ / འཇལ་ གནང་ / འཇལ་གནང་	to enter (h)	བཞེས་སྒོང་	egg (h)
ཞ་		བཞེས་ཐུག་	noodle soup (h)
ཞ་སྨྱུག་	pencil	བཞེས་སྣུམ་	oil (h)
ཞབས་ཀུག་	chair (h)	བཞེས་བག་	bread (h)
ཞལ་དཀར་	cup (h)	བཞེས་འབྲས་	rice (h)
ཞལ་པར་	telephone (h)	བཞེས་མོག་	steamed dumpling (h)
ཞལ་པར་བཏང་གནང་ / ཞལ་པར་བཏང་གནང་ / ཞལ་པར་བཏང་གནང་	to telephone (h)	བཞེས་ཚོང་	onion (h)
		བཞེས་ཚལ་	vegetable or stir-fry dish (h)
ཞི་མི་	cat	བཞེས་ཞོག་	potato (h)
ཞིམ་པོ་	tasty, delicious	བཞེས་ཁུ་མ་	orange (h)
ཞུ་ / ཞུ་ / ཞུས་	to request, to partake	བཞེས་ཀུ་	apple (h)
ཞུས་གནང་ / ཞུས་གནང་ / ཞུས་གནང་	to request, to partake (h)	**ཟ་**	
ཞེ་དྲག་	very	ཟ་ཁང་	restaurant
ཞེད་པོ་ཅིག་	very, extremely	ཟིན་པ་	reaching (before the hour)
ཞོ་	yogurt	ཟླ་ཉིན་ / ན་ཉིན་	last year
ཞོག་གོག་	potato	ཟླ་བ་	month, moon, p.n.
གཞིས་ཀ་རྩེ་	Shi-ḡa-ḏzé	གཟའ་འཁོར་	week
གཞུག་ལ་ / རྗེས་ལ་	after	གཟའ་ཉི་མ་	Sunday
གཉིས་ཅིན་	two years ago	གཟའ་པ་སངས་	Friday
གཉིས་ཅིན་ཁ་	two days after tomorrow	གཟའ་སྤེན་པ་	Saturday
		གཟའ་ཕུར་བུ་	Thursday
བཞི་	four	གཟའ་མིག་དམར་	Tuesday
		གཟའ་ཟླ་བ་	Monday

གཟའ་ལྷག་པ་	Wednesday
གཟིགས་ / གཟིགས་ / གཟིགས་	to buy (h), to see (h)
གཟིམ་ཁང་	home (h)
གཟིམ་འཁུག་ / གཟིམ་འཁུགས་ / གཟིམ་ཁུགས་	to sleep (h)
གཟིམ་སྒོ་	door (h)
གཟུགས་པོ་	body
བཟའ་ / ཟ་ / བཟས་	to eat
བཟའ་ཟླ་	spouse
བཟོ་ / བཟོ་ / བཟོས་	to make, to prepare
བཟོས་གནང་ / བཟོས་གནང་ / བཟོས་གནང་	to make, to prepare (h)

འ་

འོ་མ་	milk
འོག་ལ་	under, beneath, below

ཡ་

ཡ་གི་	that up there
ཡ་གིར་	up there
ཡག་ཉེས་	quality (lit., "good-bad")
ཡག་པོ་	good
ཡང་སྐྱར་	again
ཡང་ལྗིད་	weight (lit., "light-heavy")
ཡང་པོ་	light
ཨེ་གི་	letter
ཡེ་ཤུ་པ་	Christian
ཡོང་ / ཡོང་ / ཡོང་	to come

གཡག་ཤ་ / ཚག་ཤ་	yak meat
གཡར་ / གཡར་ / གཡར་ད་	to borrow, to lend
གཡར་གནང་ / གཡར་གནང་ / གཡར་གནང་	to borrow, to lend (h)
གཡས་	right
གཡས་ངོས་	right side
གཡས་གཡོན་ལ་	on either side of
གཡོན་	left
གཡོན་ངོས་	left side

ར་

རི་	mountain
རིང་ཐུང་	length
རིང་པོ་	long
རིན་པོ་ཆེ་	Rînboché (lit., "precious one"; an epithet for a lama)
རྔངས་བཙོས་བསྐྱོན་ / རྔངས་བཙོས་སྐྱོན་ / རྔངས་བཙོས་བསྐྱོནད་	to steam (h)
རྔངས་བཙོས་བརྒྱབ་ / རྔངས་བཙོས་རྒྱབ་ / རྔངས་བཙོས་བརྒྱབས་	to steam

ལ་

ལ་དྭགས་	Ladakh
ལམ་ཁ་	road
ལས་ཀ་	work
ལས་ཀ་བྱ་ / ལས་ཀ་བྱེད་ / ལས་ཀ་བྱས་	to work
ལས་སླ་པོ་	easy

ལུག་ཤ་   lamb meat

ཞིན་/ཞིན་/ཟུངས་   to take, to partake

ལོ་   year

ཤ་

ཤ་   meat

ཤིང་ཏོག་   fruit

ཤིང་ཏོག་ཚོང་མཁན་   fruit seller

ཤེས་/ཤེས་/ཤེས་   to know

ཤོག་བུ་²   paper

ས་

ས་ཆ་   area, place

ས་གདན་   rug

སང་དགོང་   tomorrow evening, next evening

སང་ཉིན་   tomorrow

སེམས་བཟང་པོ་   kind, good-hearted

སེར་པོ་   yellow

སོག་པོ་   Mongolian

སྲན་མ་   pea

སྲས་   boy/son (h)

སྲས་མོ་   girl/daughter (h)

སླ་པོ་   weak (with beverages)

སློབ་གྲྭ་/སློབ་གྲྭ་   school

སློབ་གྲྭ་བ་   student

སློབ་སྦྱོང་   studies

སློབ་སྦྱོང་གནང་/སློབ་སྦྱོང་གནང་/སློབ་སྦྱོང་གནང་   to study (h)

སློབ་སྦྱོང་བྱ་/སློབ་སྦྱོང་བྱེད་/སློབ་སྦྱོང་བྱས་   to study

གསད་/གསོད་/བསད་   to kill, to turn off

གསན་/གསན་/གསནད་   to hear (h)

གསར་པ་   new

གསར་པོ་   pretty new

གསར་འོག   newspaper

གསུམ་   three

གསོ་བ་   parched barley dough (h)

གསོལ་ཀུམ་   meat (h)

གསོལ་ཅོག་   table (h)

གསོལ་ཇ་   tea (h)

གསོལ་ཇ་མངར་མོ་   sweet tea (h)

གསོལ་མར་   butter (h)

གསོལ་ཚིགས་/ཞལ་ལག་   food (h)

གསོལ་ཞིབ་   ground parched barley (h)

གསོལ་ཞོ་   yogurt (h)

བསད་གནང་/བསད་གནང་/བསད་གནང་   to kill, to turn off (h)

བསམ་/སེམས་/བསམས་   to think

བསིལ་པོ་   cool

བསོད་ནམས་   merit

བསྲེག་³/སྲེག་/བསྲེགས་   to roast

བསྲེགས་གནང་/བསྲེགས་གནང་/བསྲེགས་གནང་   to roast (h)

ཏ་

ཏ་གོ/ ཏ་གོ/ ཏ་གོ	to understand
ཏ་ཅང་	very
ལྷ་ཁང་	temple
ལྷ་ས་	Hla-ša
ལྷ་སའི་སྐད་	Hla-ša dialect
ལྷགས་པ/ རླུང་	wind
ལྷགས་པ་བརྒྱབ/ ལྷགས་ པ་རྒྱབ/ ལྷགས་པ་ བརྒྱབས་	to be windy
ཕྱན་ཆུས་	together (h)

ཨ་

ཨ་ཅག་ལགས་	sister (h)
ཨ་ནེ་	Nun
ཨ་ནེའི་དགོན་པ་	nunnery
ཨ་བ་	child (h)
ཨ་མ་ལགས་	mother (h)
ཨ་མེ་རི་ཀ་	America/ American
ཨམ་	mango
ཨིན་ཇི་	English person or Westerner
ཨིན་ཇིའི་སྐད་	English language
ཨིན་ཇིའི་ལུང་པ་	England
ཨུ་རུ་སུ་	Russian

---

[1] Pronounced b̄u-gu.

[2] Pronounced šhu-gu.

[3] In Central Tibetan dialect, pronounced d̠a'.

English-Tibetan Vocabulary

(All verbs are listed under the infinitive, "to …".)

A

about	སྐོར་
accomplished the purpose [purpose-accomplished; Sanskrit: *Siddhārtha*], p.n.	དོན་གྲུབ་
after	གཞུག་ལ་/ རྗེས་ལ་
again	ཡང་སྐྱར་
ago, earlier, previously	སྔོན་ལ་
airplane	གནམ་གྲུ་
airport	གནམ་གྲུ་ཐང་
all	ཚང་མ་
America/ American	ཨ་མེ་རི་ཀ
and	དང་
and a half	དང་ཕྱེད་ཀ
apple (h)	བཞེས་ཤུ་
apple	ཀུ་ཤུ་
area, place	ས་ཆ་

B

bad	ཉེས་པོ་
bad, awful	སྡུག་ཆག
baker, bread seller	བག་ལེབ་ཚོང་མཁན་
banana	ཀེ་ལ་

bank	དངུལ་ཁང་
barber shop	སྐྲ་ཁང་
bearer of the teachings [teachings-bearer], p.n.	བསྟན་འཛིན་
beef	གླང་ཤ་
beer, barley wine (h)	མཆོད་ཆང་
beer, barley wine	ཆང་
behind, in back of	རྒྱབ་ལ་
Bhutan	འབྲུག་ཡུལ་
big, large, great	ཆེ་/ ཆེན་པོ་
black	ནག་པོ་
blue	སྔོན་པོ་
Bodh Gaya	རྡོ་རྗེ་གདན་
body (h)	སྐུ་གཟུགས་
body	གཟུགས་པོ་
book (h)	ཕྱག་དེབ་
book	དེབ་
boy/son (h)	སྲས་
boy/son	བུ་
bread (h)	བཞེས་བག
bread	བག་ལེབ་
brown	རྒྱ་སྨུག་/ སྨུག་པོ་

Buddhist text (Tibetan style, h) ཕྱག་དཔེ་

Buddhist text (Tibetan style) དཔེ་ཆ་

Buddhist ནང་པ་

butter (h) གསོལ་མར་

butter མར་

C

cabbage པད་ཚལ་

Canada ཁ་ན་ཌ་

car མོ་ཊར་

carrot གུང་ལ་ཕུག་

cat ཞི་མི་

Central Tibetan dialect དབུས་སྐད་

chair (h) ཞབས་ཁུག་

chair རྐུབ་ཀྱག་

chicken meat བྱ་ཤ་

child (h) ཨ་བ་

child ཕྲུ་གུ་[1]

China རྒྱ་ནག་

Chinese language རྒྱ་སྐད་

Chinese རྒྱ་མི་

Cho-khang ཇོ་ཁང་

Christian ཡེ་ཤུ་པ་

city, town གྲོང་ཁྱེར་

cold གྲང་མོ་

color ཚོས་མདོག་

compassion (h) ཐུགས་རྗེ་

compassion སྙིང་རྗེ་

conquering, p.n. རྣམ་རྒྱལ་

conversation (h) བཀའ་མོལ་

conversation སྐད་ཆ་

cool བསིལ་པོ་

cup (h) ཁལ་དཀར་

cup དཀར་ཡོལ་

D

Darjeeling རྡོ་རྗེ་གླིང་

date ཚེས་པ་

day after tomorrow གནངས་ཉིན་ཁ་/ནངས་ཉིན་

Delhi དི་ལི་

Dharamsala དྷ་རམ་ས་ལ་

difficult ཁག་པོ་

distant, far ཐག་རིང་པོ་

dog ཁྱི་

door (h) གཟིམ་སྒོ་

door སྒོ་

down there མ་གིར་

dream རྨི་ལམ་/གཉིད་ལམ་

Dzang dialect གཙང་སྐད་

E

early སྔ་པོ་

easy ལས་སླ་པོ་

egg (h) བཞེས་སྒོང་

egg སྒོང་

England ཨིན་ཇིའི་ལུང་པ་

English language	ཨིན་ཇིའི་སྐད་	from where (interrogative particle)	ག་ནས་
English person or Westerner	ཨིན་ཇི་	fruit	ཤིང་ཏོག་
evening	དགོང་དག/དགོང་དྲོ་	fruit seller	ཤིང་ཏོག་ཚོང་མཁན་

G

exalted activities	འཕྲིན་ལས་	Germany	འཇར་མན་
expensive	གོང་ཆེན་པོ་	girl/daughter (h)	སྲས་མོ་
far away, in the distance	རྒྱང་རིང་པོ་	girl/daughter	བུ་མོ་

F

father (h)	ཕ་ལགས་	glorious [glory-possessing], p.n.	དཔལ་ལྡན་
fearless [fear-without; used as p.n. for male only]	འཇིགས་མེད་	good fortune [fortune-good], p.n.	སྐལ་བཟང་
feeling, comfort	བདེ་སྡུག་	good luck/auspicious, p.n.	བཀྲ་ཤིས་
few, a little	ཅུང་ཅུང་	good mind [mind-good], p.n.	བློ་བཟང་
first	དང་པོ་	good	ཡག་པོ་
fish meat	ཉ་ཤ་	grape	སྐྱུན་འབྲུམ་
five	ལྔ་	great, big, large	ཆེ་/ཆེན་པོ་
flour	གྲོ་ཞིབ་	green	ལྗང་ཁུ་
flower	མེ་ཏོག་	ground parched barley (h)	གསོལ་ཞིབ་
food (h)	གསོལ་ཚིགས་/ཞལ་ལག་	ground parched barley	རྩམ་པ་
food	ཁ་ལག་	gun	མེ་མདའ་
four	བཞི་	

H

France	ཕ་རན་སི་	he/she (h)	ཁོང་
French language	ཕ་རན་སིའི་སྐད་	he	ཁོ་/ཁོ་རང་
French	ཕ་རན་སི་	healthy	བདེ་པོ་
Friday	གཟའ་པ་སངས་	healthy-happy [used as p.n. for female only]	བདེ་སྐྱིད་
friend (female)	གྲོགས་མོ་	heavy	ལྗིད་པོ་
friend (male)	གྲོགས་པོ་	
from (someone)	རྩ་ནས་	

here and there, there and back	པར་ཚུར་
here	འདིར་
Hla-ša	ལྷ་ས་
Hla-ša dialect	ལྷ་སའི་སྐད་
home (h)	གཟིམ་ཁང་
home	ནང་
honest	དྲང་པོ་
hospital	སྨན་ཁང་
hot	ཚ་པོ་
hotel, inn	མགྲོན་ཁང་
hotel, inn, hostel	གནས་ཚང་
hour, o'clock, watch, clock	ཆུ་ཚོད་
how much, how many	ག་ཚོད་ / ག་ཚད་

I

I	ང་
in front of	མདུན་ལ་
in this way, such (lit., "this-like")	འདི་འདྲ་ / འདི་འདྲས་
in, inside	ནང་ལ་
India	རྒྱ་གར་
Indian	རྒྱ་གར་བ་
inexpensive	གོང་ཁེ་པོ་ / ཁེ་པོ་

J

| just right | ཏག་ཏག་ |

K

| Kathmandu | ཀ་ཏ་མན་ཌུ་ |
| Kham dialect | ཁམས་སྐད་ |

| kind, good-hearted | སེམས་བཟང་པོ་ |

L

Ladakh	ལ་དྭགས་
lake	མཚོ་
lama	བླ་མ་
lamb meat	ལུག་ཤ་
lamp	བཞུ་མར་
large, big, great	ཆེན་པོ་
last night	མདང་ས་དགོང་
last year	ན་ཉིན་ / ན་ཉིན་
late	ཕྱི་པོ་
left	གཡོན་
left side	གཡོན་ངོས་
length	རིང་ཐུང་
let's (mild imperative)	དོ་
letter (h)	ཕྱག་བྲིས་
letter	ཡི་གེ་
library	དཔེ་མཛོད་ཁང་
light	ཡང་པོ་
little	ཅུང་ཅུང་
long	རིང་པོ་
long life [life-long], p.n.	ཚེ་རིང་
lotus [transliteration of Sanskrit *padma*], p.n.	པད་མ་

M

magazine	ཚག་པར་
mango	ཨམ་
market	ཁྲོམ་

meat (h)	གསོལ་ཀུ་མེ་	noodle soup (h)	བཞེས་ཐུག
meat	ཤ་	noodle soup	ཐུག་པ་
merit	བསོད་ནམས་	noon	ཉིན་གུང་
milk (h)	ཆབ་ཞོ་	Nun	ཨ་ནེ་
milk	འོ་མ་	nunnery	ཨ་ནེའི་དགོན་པ་
minute	སྐར་མ་		
monastery	དགོན་པ་	**O**	
monastic college	གྲྭ་ཚང་	ocean [vast-lake], p.n.	རྒྱ་མཚོ་
Monday	གཟའ་ཟླ་བ་	oil (h)	བཞེས་སྣུམ་
Mongolian	སོག་པོ་	oil	སྣུམ་
monk	གྲྭ་པ་	old	རྙིང་པ་
month	ཟླ་བ་	on either side of	གཡས་གཡོན་ལ་
moon, p.n.	ཟླ་བ་	on, on top of	སྟེང་ལ་
mother (h)	ཨ་མ་ལགས་	one	གཅིག
mountain	རི་	onion (h)	བཞེས་ཙོང་
movie theater	གློག་བརྙན་ཁང་	onion	ཙོང་
much,many, a lot	མང་པོ་	orange (h)	བཞེས་ལུ་མ་
Muslim	ཁ་ཆེ་	orange	ཚ་ལུ་མ་
		over here	ཚུར་
N		over there	ཕར་
name (h)	མཚན་	over there, there	ཕ་གིར་
name	མིང་		
near, close	ཐག་ཉེ་པོ་	**P**	
near, beside	འཁྲིས་ལ་	paper (h)	ཕྱག་ཤོག
new	གསར་པ་	paper	ཤོག་བུ་²
newspaper	གསར་ཤོག	parched barley dough (h)	གསོལ་བ་
next year	དུས་སང་	parched barley dough	རྩམ་པ་
nomad	འབྲོག་པ་	parents	ཕ་མ་
		pea	སྲན་མ་

pen (h)	ཕྱག་སྨྱུག	rest	ངལ་གསོ་
pen	སྨྱུ་གུ	restaurant	ཟ་ཁང་
pencil	ཞ་སྨྱུག	rice (h)	བཞེས་འབྲས་
person, man	མི་	rice	འབྲས་
pleasant, comfortable (h)	སྐྱིད་པོ་	rich	ཕྱུག་པོ་
pleasant, comfortable	སྐྱིད་པོ་	right	གཡས་
pork	ཕག་ཤ་	right side	གཡས་ངོས་
post office	སྦྲག་ཁང་	Rînboché (lit., "precious one"; an epithet for a lama)	རིན་པོ་ཆེ་
potato (h)	བཞེས་ཞོག་		
potato	ཞོག་གོག་	road	ལམ་ཁ་
power of speech [speech-power], p.n.	ངག་དབང་	rug	ས་གདན་
		Russian	ཨུ་རུ་སུ་
presentation scarf	ཁ་བཏགས་		
pretty new	གསར་ར་པོ་	**S**	
pretty old	རྙིང་པོ་	salt (h)	ལྕགས་ཚྭ་
previously	སྔོན་མ་	salt	ཚྭ་
price (h)	ལྕགས་གོང་	Saturday	གཟའ་སྤེན་པ་
price	གོང་	savioress (a goddess) [Sanskrit: *Tārā*; used as p.n. for female only]	སྒྲོལ་མ་
prison	བཙོན་ཁང་		
Q			
quality (lit., "good-bad")	ཡག་ཉེས་	school	སློབ་གྲྭ་ / སློབ་གྲྭ་
quantity (lit., "many-few"	མང་ཉུང་	scroll painting	ཐང་ག་
R		she/he (h)	ཁོང་
rain	ཆར་པ་	she	མོ་ / མོ་རང་
reaching (before the hour)	ཟིན་པ་	Shi-ga-dzé	གཞིས་ཀ་རྩེ་
really	དངོས་གནས་	short	ཐུང་ཐུང་
red	དམར་པོ་	short time ago, a	ད་གིན་
		Sikkim	འབྲས་ལྗོངས་
		sister (h)	ཨ་ཅག་ལགས་

six	དྲུག	table	ཅོག་ཙེ
size (lit., "big-small")	ཆེ་ཆུང་	tasty, delicious (h)	སྙོ་པོ
small	ཆུང་ཆུང་	tasty, delicious	ཞིམ་པོ
soda, soft drink (h)	ཆབ་མངར་མོ	tavern	ཆང་ཁང་
soda, soft drink	ཆུ་མངར་མོ	tea (h)	གསོལ་ཇ
soldier	དམག་མི	tea	ཇ
some time ago	ཁ་སང་	tea house, tea stall	ཇ་ཁང་
some, several	ཁ་ཤས་/འགའ་ཤས་	teacher	དགེ་རྒན
sour	སྐྱུར་མོ	teaching of the Muni [Muni-teaching], p.n.	ཐུབ་བསྟན
spouse (h)	སྐུ་ཟླ	telephone (h)	ཞལ་པར་
spouse	བཟའ་ཟླ	telephone	ཁ་པར
steamed dumpling with no filling	སྐྱིང་མོག་མོག/སྐྱིང་མོག	temperature (lit., "hot-cold")	ཚ་གྲང་
steamed dumpling (h)	བཞེས་མོག	temple	ལྷ་ཁང་
steamed dumpling	མོག་མོག	thank you	ཐུགས་རྗེ་ཆེ
store	ཚོང་ཁང་	that down there	མ་གི
stroll, walk	ཆམ་ཆམ	that over there	ཕ་གི
strong (with beverages)	གར་པོ	that up there	ཡ་གི
student	སློབ་གྲྭ་བ	that	དེ
studies	སློབ་སྦྱོང་	then	དེ་ནས་
sugar	བྱེ་མ་ཀ་ར	these	འདི་ཚོ
sun, p.n.	ཉི་མ	they (f/m) (h)	ཁོང་ཚོ
Sunday	གཟའ་ཉི་མ	they (f)	མོ་རང་ཚོ
sweet	མངར་མོ	they (m)	ཁོ་ཚོ/ཁོ་རང་ཚོ
sweet tea (h)	གསོལ་ཇ་མངར་མོ	this	འདི
sweet tea	ཇ་མངར་མོ	those	དེ་ཚོ
		three	གསུམ

T

table (h)	གསོལ་ཅོག

thunderbolt [Sanskrit: *vajra*], p.n.	རྡོ་རྗེ་
Thursday	གཟའ་ཕུར་བུ་
Tibet	བོད་
Tibetan	བོད་པ་
Tibetan language	བོད་སྐད་
Tibetan tea	བོད་ཇ་
to (someone), at	རུ་ལ་
to agree (h)	མཐུན་གནང་ / མཐུན་ གནང་ / མཐུན་གནང་
to agree	མཐུན་ / མཐུན་ / མཐུན་
to arrive (h)	འབྱོར་གནང་ / འབྱོར་ གནང་ / འབྱོར་གནང་ ཕེབས་འབྱོར་གནང་ / ཕེབས་འབྱོར་གནང་ / ཕེབས་འབྱོར་གནང་
to arrive	འབྱོར་ / འབྱོར་ / འབྱོརད་ བསླེབ་ / སླེབ་ / བསླེབས་
to ask (h)	བཀའ་འདྲི་གནང་ / བཀའ་ འདྲི་གནང་ / བཀའ་ འདྲི་གནང་
to ask	སྐད་ཆ་འདྲི་ / སྐད་ཆ་དྲི་ / སྐད་ཆ་དྲིས་
to be correct, to be okay	འགྲིག་ / འགྲིག་ / འགྲིགས་
to be sick (h)	བསྙུང་ / སྙུང་ / བསྙུངས་
to be sick	ན་ / ན་ / ན་
to be windy	ལྷགས་པ་བརྒྱབ་ / ལྷགས་ པ་རྒྱབ་ / ལྷགས་པ་ བརྒྱབས་
to borrow, to lend (h)	གཡར་གནང་ / གཡར་ གནང་ / གཡར་གནང་
to borrow, to lend	གཡར་ / གཡར་ / གཡརད་
to bring, to carry (h)	སྐྱེལ་ / སྐྱེལ་ / བསྐྱལ་
to bring, to carry	ཁྱེར་ / འཁྱེར་ / ཁྱེརད་
to build, to make, to put (h)	བསྐྲུན་ / སྐྲུན་ / བསྐྲུནད་
to build, to make, to put	བརྒྱབ་ / རྒྱབ་ / བརྒྱབས་
to buy (h)	གཉེགས་ / གཉེགས་ / གཉེགས་
to buy	ཉོ་ / ཉོ་ / ཉོས་
to catch cold (h)	ཆམ་པ་བསྐྱུན་ / ཆམས་ པ་སྐྱུན་ / ཆམས་པ་ བསྐྱུནད་
to catch cold	ཆམས་པ་བརྒྱབ་ / ཆམས་ པ་རྒྱབ་ / ཆམས་པ་ བརྒྱབས་
to combine, to add	བསྡོམ་ / སྡོམ་ / བསྡོམས་
to come, to go (h)	ཕེབས་ / ཕེབས་ / ཕེབས་
to come	ཡོང་ / ཡོང་ / ཡོང་
to divide, to share	བགོ་ / བགོ་ / བགོས་
to do (h)	གནང་ / གནང་ / གནང་
to do	བྱ་ / བྱེད་ / བྱས་
to dream (h)	རྨི་ལམ་བཏང་གནང་ / རྨི་ ལམ་བཏང་གནང་ / རྨི་ ལམ་བཏང་གནང་
to dream	རྨི་ལམ་གཏང་ / རྨི་ལམ་ གཏང་ / རྨི་ལམ་བཏང་
to drink (h)	མཆོད་ / མཆོད་ / མཆོད་
to drink	བཏུང་ / འཐུང་ / བཏུངས་

to drive a car (h)	མོ་ཊོར་བཏང་གནང་། / མོ་ཊོར་བཏང་གནང་། / མོ་ཊོར་བཏང་གནང་	to kill, to turn off (h)	བསད་གནང་། / བསད་གནང་། / བསད་གནང་
to drive a car	མོ་ཊོར་གཏང་། / མོ་ཊོར་གཏོང་། / མོ་ཊོར་བཏང་	to kill, to turn off	གསད། / གསོད། / བསད
to eat (h)	མཆོད། / མཆོད། / མཆོད	to know (h)	མཁྱེན། / མཁྱེན། / མཁྱེནད
to eat	བཟའ། / ཟ། / བཟས	to know	ཤེས། / ཤེས། / ཤེས
to enter (h)	འཛུལ་གནང་། / འཛུལ་གནང་། / འཛུལ་གནང་	to know someone (h)	ངོ་མཁྱེན། / ངོ་མཁྱེན། / ངོ་མཁྱེནད
to enter	འཛུལ། / འཛུལ། / འཛུལ	to know someone	ངོ་ཤེས། / ངོ་ཤེས། / ངོ་ཤེས
to feel cold (h)	སྐུ་བསིལ། / སྐུ་བསིལ། / སྐུ་བསིལ	to make, to prepare (h)	བཟོས་གནང་། / བཟོས་གནང་། / བཟོས་གནང་
to feel cold	འཁྱག / འཁྱག / འཁྱགས	to make, to prepare	བཟོ། / བཟོ། / བཟོས
to finish (h)	འགྲུབ། / འགྲུབ། / གྲུབ	to meet (h)	མཇལ། / མཇལ། / མཇལད
to finish	ཚར། / ཚར། / ཚརད		མཇལ་གནང་། / མཇལ་གནང་། / མཇལ་གནང་
to fry (foods), to parch (barley) (h)	བརྔོས་གནང་། / བརྔོས་གནང་། / བརྔོས་གནང་	to meet	ཕྲད། / ཕྲད། / ཕྲད
to fry (foods), to parch (barley)	བརྔོ། / རྔོ། / བརྔོས	to need, to want (h)	དགོས་གནང་། / དགོས་གནང་། / དགོས་གནང་
to give, to do (h)	གནང་། / གནང་། / གནང་	to need, to want	དགོས། / དགོས། / དགོས
to give	བསྟེར། / སྟེར། / བསྟེརད	to offer (h)	ཕུལ་གནང་། / ཕུལ་གནང་། / ཕུལ་གནང་
to give	སྤྲད། / སྤྲོད། / སྤྲད	to offer	འབུལ། / འབུལ། / ཕུལ
to go, to come (h)	ཕེབས། / ཕེབས། / ཕེབས	to pour (h)	བླུགས་གནང་། / བླུགས་གནང་། / བླུགས་གནང་
to go	འགྲོ། / འགྲོ། / ཕྱིན	to pour	བླུག / བླུག / བླུགས
to hear (h)	གསན། / གསན། / གསནད	to practice, to train, to learn (h)	སྦྱངས་གནང་། / སྦྱངས་གནང་། / སྦྱངས་གནང་
to hear, to understand	གོ། / གོ། / གོ		
to ignite, to turn on (h)	སྤྲ་གནང་། / སྤྲ་གནང་། / སྤྲ་གནང་		
to ignite, to turn on	སྤྲ། / སྤྲོ། / སྤྲརད	to practice, to train, to learn	སྦྱང་། / སྦྱོང་། / སྦྱངས

to rain	ཆར་པ་གཏང་། / ཆར་པ་ གཏོང་། / ཆར་པ་བཏང་	to sit, to stay (h)	བཞུགས། / བཞུགས། / བཞུགས་
to read (h)	ལྫགས་ཀློག་གནང་། / ལྫགས་ ཀློག་གནང་། / ལྫགས་ཀློག་ གནང་	to sit, to stay	བསྡད། / སྡོད། / བསྡད་
		to sleep (h)	གཟིམ་འཁུག / གཟིམ་ འཁུགས། / གཟིམ་ཁུགས་
to read	བཀླག / ཀློག / བཀླགས་	to sleep	གཉིད་འཁུག / གཉིད་ འཁུགས། / གཉིད་ཁུགས་
to reduce, to subtract	ཕྲིན། / འཕྲིན། / ཕྲིནད་		
to remember (h)	དྲན་གནང་། / དྲན་གནང་། / དྲནད་གནང་	to steam (h)	རླངས་བཙོས་བསྐྱོན། / རླངས་བཙོས་སྐྱོན། / རླངས་བཙོས་བསྐྱོནད་
to remember	དྲན། / དྲན། / དྲནད་		
to request, to partake (h)	ཞུས་གནང་། / ཞུས་གནང་། / ཞུས་གནང་	to steam	རླངས་བཙོས་བརྒྱབ། / རླངས་བཙོས་རྒྱབ། / རླངས་བཙོས་བརྒྱབས་
to request, to partake	ཞུ། / ཞུ། / ཞུས་		
to rest (h)	ངལ་གསོ་བསྐྱོན། / ངལ་ གསོ་སྐྱོན། / ངལ་གསོ་ བསྐྱོནད་	to study (h)	སློབ་སྦྱོང་གནང་། / སློབ་སྦྱོང་ གནང་། / སློབ་སྦྱོང་གནང་
		to study	སློབ་སྦྱོང་བྱ། / སློབ་སྦྱོང་ བྱེད། / སློབ་སྦྱོང་བྱས་
to rest	ངལ་གསོ་བརྒྱབ། / ངལ་ གསོ་རྒྱབ། / ངལ་གསོ་ བརྒྱབས་	to take, to partake (h)	བཞེས། / བཞེས། / བཞེས་
		to take, to partake	བླང་། / ལེན། / བླངས་
to roast (h)	བསྲེགས་³གནང་། / བསྲེགས་གནང་། / བསྲེགས་གནང་		ལེན། / ལེན། / བླངས་
		to telephone (h)	ཁལ་པར་བཏང་གནང་། / ཁལ་པར་བཏང་གནང་། / ཁལ་པར་བཏང་གནང་
to roast	བསྲེག / སྲེག / བསྲེགས་		
to see (h)	གཟིགས། / གཟིགས། / གཟིགས་	to telephone	ཁ་པར་གཏང་། / ཁ་པར་ གཏོང་། / ཁ་པར་བཏང་
to see	མཐོང་། / མཐོང་། / མཐོང་	to think (h)	དགོངས། / དགོངས། / དགོངས་
to sell (h)	ཚོང་བསྐྱོན། / ཚོང་སྐྱོན། / ཚོང་བསྐྱོནད་	to think	བསམ། / སེམས། / བསམས་
to sell	བཙོང་། / འཚོང་། / བཙོངས་	to understand (h)	མཁྱིན། / མཁྱིན། / མཁྱིནད་

to understand	ཉ་གོ། / ཉ་གོ། / ཉ་གོ།	vegetable or stir-fry dish (h)	བཞེས་ཚལ་
to work (h)	ཕྱག་ལས་གནང་ / ཕྱག་ལས་གནང་ / ཕྱག་ལས་གནང་	vegetable or stir-fry dish	ཚལ་
to work	ལས་ཀ་བྱ / ལས་ཀ་བྱེད་ / ལས་ཀ་བྱས་	very	ཞེ་དྲག
		very	ཧ་ཅང་
to write, to paint, to draw (h)	བྲིས་གནང་ / བྲིས་གནང་ / བྲིས་གནང་	very, exceptionally	དཔེ་
to write, to paint, to draw	བྲི་ / འབྲི་ / བྲིས་	very, extremely	ཞིད་པོ་ཅིག

W

today	དེ་རིང་	water (h)	ཆབ་
together (h)	ཐུན་ཅུས་	water	ཆུ་
together	མཉམ་དུ་	we	ང་ཚོ། / ང་རང་ཚོ་
tomorrow	སང་ཉིན་	we two, the two of us (lit., "I" and "two")	ང་གཉིས་
tomorrow evening, next evening	སང་དགོང་	weak (with beverages)	སླ་པོ་
tonight	དོ་དགོང་	weather	གནམ་གཤིས་
Tuesday	གཟའ་མིག་དམར་	Wednesday	གཟའ་ལྷག་པ་
two days after tomorrow	གཞིས་ཉིན་ཁ་	week	བདུན་ཕྲག
two	གཉིས་	week	གཟའ་འཁོར་
two years ago	གཞིས་ཉིན་	weight (lit., "light-heavy")	ཡང་ལྗིད་

U

		well then (lit., "if done")	བྱས་ན་
under, beneath, below	འོག་ལ་	what (interrogative particle)	ག་རེ་
unit of money (dollar, rupee, franc, etc.)	སྒོར་མོ་	when (interrogative particle)	ག་དུས་
up there	ཡ་གིར་	where (interrogative particle)	ག་པར་

V

		White Tārā ["Tārā-white"; used as a personal name for female only]	སྒྲོལ་དཀར་
vacation	གུང་སེང་		
various	འདྲ་མི་འདྲ་	white	དཀར་པོ་

wind	ལྷགས་པ་/ རླུང་
window	སྒེ་ཁུང་
woman	བུད་མེད་/ སྐྱེ་དམན་
work (h)	ཕྱག་ལས་
work	ལས་ཀ་

Y

yak meat	གཡག་ཤ་/ ཚག་ཤ་
year	ལོ་
yellow	སེར་པོ་
yesterday	ཁ་ས་
yogurt (h)	གསོལ་ཞོ་
yogurt	ཞོ་
you (h singular)	ཁྱེད་རང་
you (singular)	ཁྱོད་རང་
you (h plural)	ཁྱེད་རང་ཚོ་
you (plural)	ཁྱོད་རང་ཚོ་/ ཁྱོད་ཚོ་

---

[1] Pronounced b̄u-gu.

[2] Pronounced s̄hu-gu.

[3] Pronounced ḍa'.

Grammar

In this section the grammatical points scattered throughout the fifteen units are repeated, with a little additional material, under their respective parts of speech.

PROPER NAMES

Many Tibetan names can be used for persons of either gender. Moreover, most Tibetans, lay government officials being the main exception, do not use a family name as a last name and do not distinguish between "first" and "last" names in the way that Europeans and Americans do.[1] Tibetans usually have two names, like འཕྲིན་ལས་རྣམ་རྒྱལ་. Like most words in Tibetan, names tend to be disyllabic (two syllables), and any name can be in either the first position or in the second position. Although many Tibetans in the West have adopted the custom of referring to people by first name only, frequently both names are used, without implying the same degree of formality that is the case when using first and last names in a Western context. One traditional way of shortening a name, as with friends, is to use the first and third syllables of the pair of names. Hence འཕྲིན་ལས་རྣམ་རྒྱལ་, for instance, shortens to འཕྲིན་རྣམ་. Indeed, using the first and third syllables is a typical way of making abbreviations in Tibetan. Further, although names are not rigidly gender specific, it is often possible to tell from a name whether someone is male or female and also whether they are either a layperson or a monk or nun. Most Tibetan names have a meaning reflecting the close link between Buddhism and Tibetan culture. Buddhist virtues, good luck wishes, and the days of the week, usually reflecting the day on which a child was born, are commonly used as names. For instance, ཡེ་ཤེས་ means "wisdom". Tibetans commonly add the syllable ལགས་ after a person's name when speaking to or about someone—for example, ཡེ་ཤེས་ལགས་ or བསོད་ནམས་ལགས་—to express affection and respect. For drills see Unit 4.5-4.20; for drills on asking what someone's name is, see Unit 14.5-14.8.

---

[1] This is not to say that Tibetans do not distinguish between family and personal names.

The syllable ལགས་ is practically omnipresent. By itself, this particle is difficult to translate, for it sometimes conveys the sense of "yes", at other times may be used (in a rather informal way) like "Huh?", and at the very least acknowledges the other person's statement. It is put before almost any response as an indication of politeness and is put after any name for the same reason.

NOUNS

AGENT NOUNS

In Unit 7, the dialogue ends with Ḏa-s̄hí saying ཤིང་ཏོག་ཚོང་མཁན་ག་པར་འདུག ("Where is the fruit seller?"), and Ṯön-ḏup replying ཕ་གིར་འདུག ("Over there"). The word ཚོང་ is the verb "to sell"; the particle མཁན་ turns ཚོང་ into an agent noun; thus, ཚོང་མཁན་ means "seller" or "vendor", as when in the dialogue Ḏa-s̄hí asks ཤིང་ཏོག་ཚོང་མཁན་ག་པར་འདུག ("Where is the fruit seller?"). Affixing མཁན་ to a verb is one of the more common ways of making an agent noun from a verb. For instance, ཉེ་མཁན་ means "buyer", and གཉེགས་མཁན་, འགྲོ་མཁན་, and ཕེབས་མཁན་ mean "buyer" (h), "goer", and "goer" (h), respectively. For drills see Unit 7.32-7.36.

ADDING ཁང་

The names for many businesses, offices, and so forth are formed by adding the syllable ཁང་ to a noun or a verb. The word ཁང་པ་ by itself means "house" or "building", and in these compounds it has the sense of "house of...", as in ཟ་ཁང་ "house of eating" or "restaurant"; ཚོང་ཁང་ "house of selling" or "shop"; and སྨན་ཁང་ "house of medicine" or "hospital". See Unit 7.

NOMINALIZATION WITH པ་ AND བ་

Adding པ་ or བ་ to the word for an activity, object, or institution causes it to indicate a person associated with that phenomenon. For instance, སློབ་གྲྭ་ means "school", and adding བ་ to སློབ་གྲྭ་ forms the word for student, སློབ་གྲྭ་བ་. Frequently the relationship between the person and the thing is one in which the person possesses the thing. For instance, ཞིང་ means "field" and ཞིང་པ་ means "one who has a field", i.e., "farmer". See Unit 13.60.

HONORIFICS

Tibetan uses both common forms and honorific or more polite forms of address. These honorific forms occur for nouns, pronouns, adjectives, and verbs. Basically, honorifics show respect for equals and superiors and hence should be used in almost all situations; therefore, a good rule of thumb is to use them whenever either directly addressing someone or talking about someone else. Because they do express respect, polite self-effacement also demands that one not use them when referring to oneself. The implications of this in a conversation are shown in the first two lines of the Unit 6 dialogue. The question ག་པར་ཕེབས་ཀ ("Where are you going?") is asked using the honorific form of the verb "to go" (ཕེབས་) and is answered using the non-honorific form (འགྲོ). It is easier when discussing a third party; the question form would be ཁོང་ག་པར་ཕེབས་ཀྱི་རེད ("Where will she/ he go?"), and the answer would be given still using the honorific ཁྲོམ་ལ་ཕེབས་ཀྱི་རེད ("She/ he will go to the market").

Honorific words are either entirely different from the non-honorific equivalent, as in གསོལ་གྱུམ་ ("meat" h) and ཤ་ ("meat"), or combine part of the non-honorific word with an honorific particle, as in ཕྱག་དེབ་ ("book" h), which combines དེབ་ ("book") with ཕྱག་ (honorific of ལག་པ་ "hand"). Other frequent honorific particles are བཞེས་ ("take", "partake" h), used to form the honorific of many foods such as བཞེས་ཚལ་ ("vegetable" h) and བཞེས་འབྲས་ ("rice" h), and གནང་ (honorific of བྱེད་ "to do"), as in ཀློག་གློག་གནང་ ("to read" h) and many other verbs. The honorific is not a separate language, and learning it is considerably simpler than having to learn two different words for each noun, verb, and adjective since many honorifics are formed by combining the non-honorific word with an honorific particle.

In Unit 7, བཟའ་ and འཐུང་ are introduced as non-honorific terms for eating and drinking, respectively, and མཆོད་ serves as the honorific term for both eating and drinking. In Unit 11, it is stressed that one may use honorific terms for other people but never for oneself alone. Thus, Sö'-nam asks ཁྱེད་རང་ག་རེ་མཆོད་ཀ ("What will you eat/drink?" h), to which Dé-ğyi' replies ང་མངར་མོ་འཐུང་གི་ཡིན ("I will drink sweet tea"). Similarly, Sö'-nam uses ཞལ་ལག་, the honorific term for food, to ask Dé-ğyi' whether or not the food is tasty. However, in his answer ཞིམ་པོ་འདུག ("It is tasty") Sö'-nam uses ཞིམ་པོ་, the non-honorific term for "tasty", rather than ཞྱོ་པོ་, the honorific term, because he is speaking in reference to himself. Still, when telling one's hosts how delicious their food is, one would use the honorific.

PRONOUNS

The basic personal pronouns are ང་ ("I"), ཁྱེད་རང་ ("you" h), and ཁོང་ ("she" or "he" h). The latter two, ཁྱེད་རང་ and ཁོང་, are honorific forms. Pronouns are made plural by the addition of the particle ཚོ, making ང་ཚོ་ ("we"), ཁྱེད་རང་ཚོ་ ("you" h), and ཁོང་ཚོ་ ("they" h).

Basic Pronouns			
Singular		*Plural*	
ང་ or ང་རང་	I	ང་ཚོ་ or ང་རང་ཚོ་	we
ཁྱེད་རང་	you (h)	ཁྱེད་རང་ཚོ་	you (h)
ཁོང་	she/he (h)	ཁོང་ཚོ་	they (m/f) (h)

The first person plural pronoun ང་རང་ཚོ་ tends to include the person to whom one is speaking into the unit of "we" whereas ང་ཚོ་ tends to exclude that person.

Alternative personal pronouns. There are also alternative non-honorific personal pronouns for the second and third persons; these are ཁྱེད་རང་ ("you"),[1] ཁོ་ or ཁོ་རང་ ("he"), and མོ་ or མོ་རང་ ("she"). Again, the plural is formed by adding ཚོ to make ཁྱེད་རང་ཚོ་ ("you"),[2] ཁོ་ཚོ་, and ཁོ་རང་ཚོ་ ("they");[3] also མོ་རང་ཚོ་ is "they" (f) but is rarely used. The pronoun ཁོ་ཚོ་ is nasalized so that it is pronounced "khon tso".

The word རང་ means "self". However, when added to pronouns, it does not change their basic meaning; ང་ and ང་རང་ both mean "I". Adding རང་ to a pronoun puts a bit more emphasis on it, but the distinction is subtle. To shift the meaning, for instance, from "I" to "I myself", it is necessary to add a second རང་; hence, ང་རང་རང་ means "I myself".

In the Hla-śa dialect in general, the non-honorific pronouns are used infrequently, their usage reserved mainly for children or in cases of clear social inequality. The alternative pronouns are all non-honorific:

---

[1] The second person singular pronoun ཁྱེད without རང་ is seldom used in the Hla-śa dialect.

[2] The second person plural pronoun ཁྱེད་ཚོ་ without རང་ is seldom used in the Hla-śa dialect; when it is used, it is nasalized so that it is pronounced "khyön tso".

[3] Some Central Tibetans say that these terms are used only for males, whereas others say that these are used for both males and females.

Alternative Pronouns			
Singular		*Plural*	
ཁྱད་རང་	you	ཁྱད་རང་ཚོ་ or ཁྱད་ཚོ་	you
ཁོ་ or ཁོ་རང་	he	ཁོ་ཚོ་ or ཁོ་རང་ཚོ་	they
མོ་ or མོ་རང་	she	མོ་རང་ཚོ་	they

Notice that the above chart has no first person singular, since one always uses non-honorifics to refer to oneself. Also, note that some Central Tibetans advocate not using ཁོ་རང་ཚོ་ and མོ་རང་ཚོ་.

As in the sentence in the dialogue in Unit 6, ང་གཉིས་མཉམ་དུ་ཕེབས་དོ། ("Let's go together"), singular pronouns, such as ང་ ("I"), are made dual by the use of the number two (གཉིས་).

CASES

NOMINATIVE

In Unit 7 Ḍa-shí's answer ང་ཤིང་ཏོག་ཉི་གི་ཡིན། ("I'll buy fruit") introduces an important construction, the treatment of the direct object of a verb of action. Fruit (ཤིང་ཏོག་) serves as the direct object of ཉི་ ("to buy"). Here, ཤིང་ཏོག་ is an instance of the first grammatical case, called མིང་ཙམ་, which means "just the name"; as the term implies, no grammatical particles are affixed to the noun or pronoun in question. The མིང་ཙམ་ case is roughly equivalent to the nominative case in English grammar, and words in མིང་ཙམ་ in Tibetan perform many of the functions of words in the nominative in English. For instance, words in the མིང་ཙམ་ case can serve as the subject of the verb "to be", as ང་ ("I") does in the sentence ང་བོད་པ་ཡིན། ("I am a Tibetan"); they can serve as predicate nominatives, as བོད་པ་ ("Tibetan") does in the sentence ང་བོད་པ་ཡིན། ("I am a Tibetan"), and they can serve as agents of verbs of motion, living, eating/ drinking, and thinking, as ང་ does in the sentence ང་ཁྲོམ་ལ་འགྲོ་གི་ཡིན། ("I will go to the market" or "I am going to the market"). Agents of other verbs are placed in the instrumental case, and the object of the verb is placed in མིང་ཙམ་ (the nominative case), such as in ཁོས་ཤིང་ཏོག་ཉི་གི་རེད། ("He will buy fruit"). It is important to understand that Tibetan does not have separate active and passive verb forms. Therefore, the sentence ཁོས་ཤིང་ཏོག་ཉི་གི་རེད། can be translated into English either through an active construction, "He will buy fruit," or a passive construction, "The fruit will be bought by him."[1]

ACCUSATIVE

In Unit Four, we see the phrase ཁྲོམ་ལ་ in the sentence ང་ཁྲོམ་ལ་འགྲོ་གི་ཡིན། ("I will go to the market"). In the terms of English grammar, we would say that ལ་ ("to") functions as a preposition in that context and that ལ་ in combination with ཁྲོམ་ ("the market") forms a prepositional phrase meaning "to the market". However, since the Tibetan equivalents of English prepositions are placed *after* the noun they complement rather than *before* them, they are called "*post*positional particles" or case endings. In this instance, ཁྲོམ་ལ་ is in the accusative case because the case ending ལ་ indicates a destination.

The particle ལ་ and its equivalents—སུ་ , རུ་ , ཏུ་ , དུ་ , ན་ , and ར་—have a number of different usages in Tibetan; they mark the accusative, dative, and locative cases as well as the adverbial accusative. An important usage introduced in Unit 6 is its use as a mark for the destination of the verb "to go"; that is, ལ་ indicates the place to which someone or something is going—one of the usages of the accusative. For drills see Unit 9.26-9.30.

The other main usage of the accusative is as the object of the verb when this is not in the nominative. Here is a chart showing these seven endings and the suffixes with which they are used.

Suffix	Ending
ས་	སུ་
ག་ བ་ or extra suffix ད་	ཏུ་
ང་ ད་ ན་ མ་ ར་ ལ་	དུ་
འ་ or no suffix	རུ་ or ར་

Spoken Tibetan, for the most part, just uses ལ་ since it may be employed after any suffix. Sometimes ར་ substitutes for ལ་ as, for instance, when the word ལྷ་ས་ ("Hla-śa") becomes ལྷ་སར་ instead of ལྷ་ས་ལ་. In other words, if the destination indicated has no final suffix, as with ལྷ་ས་, then the particle ར་ can be added to the end of the word. When this occurs, the ར་ is not strongly pronounced; rather, it lengthens the vowel.

---

[1] Note that Tibetan allows for other word orders, such as ཤིང་ཏོག་ཁོས་ཉོ་གི་རེད།, to express changes in emphasis.

INSTRUMENTAL

The dialogue in Unit 7 indirectly introduces one of the most common Tibetan constructions, the instrumental case. When T̲ön-d̲up asks D̲a-s̲hí what he is going to buy, he says ཁྱེད་རང་ ག་རེ་གཉིགས་ཀྱི་ཡིན་པ| ("What will you buy?" h). Also, when D̲a-s̲hí answers he is going to buy fruit, he says ང་ཤིང་ཏོག་ཉོ་གི་ཡིན| ("I'll buy fruit"). Technically, T̲ön-d̲up should have said ཁྱེད་རང་གིས་ག་རེ་གཉིགས་ཀྱི་ཡིན་པ| , and D̲a-s̲hí should have answered ངས་ཤིང་ཏོག་ཉོ་གི་ཡིན| . Adding གིས་ to ཁྱེད་རང་ puts ཁྱེད་རང་ into the third grammatical case, called བྱེད་སྒྲ་, the "term of the agent" or the instrumental case. Adding ས་ to the suffixless ང་ puts ང་ into the third case. The instrumental is used to mark the agent or the means of an action. Here is a chart showing the five བྱེད་སྒྲ་ and the suffixes with which they are used.

Suffix	Ending
ད་བ་ས་	ཀྱིས་
ག་ང་	གིས་
ན་མ་ར་ལ་	གྱིས་
འ་ or no suffix	(འི་)ས་ or ཡིས་[1]

Most verbs of action require that a བྱེད་སྒྲ་ be affixed to their agents, but as can be seen from the sentences in the dialogue in Unit 7, they are frequently dropped in common usage. The rules for this are difficult to formulate, but བྱེད་སྒྲ་ are almost always omitted in the first person future and in questions in the second person future, as is seen in the first two lines of the Unit 7 dialogue. In the second person declarative and in the third person declarative and interrogative, the བྱེད་སྒྲ་ is generally used. Other verbs such as verbs of motion, living, eating/ drinking, and thinking do not call for a བྱེད་སྒྲ་ . Thus, in the dialogue in Unit 6, instrumental particles were not used in the sentences ཁྱེད་རང་ག་པར་ཕེབས་ཀ| ("Where will you go" or "Where are you going?" h) and ང་ཁྲོམ་ལ་འགྲོ་གི་ཡིན| ("I'll go to the market" or "I'm going to the market") because ཕེབས་ and འགྲོ་ are verbs of motion.

Indeed, the logic underlying the use and omission of the instrumental case (བྱེད་སྒྲ་) in spoken Tibetan is difficult to pin down. There are many occasions when the rule for literary Tibetan would call for an instrumental case particle but in conversation most people, including the well-educated, do not use it. For instance, it is not unusual to hear someone say, ང་

---

[1] In literary Tibetan, ཡིས་ sometimes is used when there is no suffix, but it rarely occurs in the spoken language.

ཀླུ་གི་ཡོད། ("I am looking at it"), even though ངས་ཀླུ་གི་ཡོད། is more proper. The verb ཤེས་ ("to know") and its honorific form མཁྱེན་ are examples of a verb that formally takes its agent in the instrumental case but in actual spoken Tibetan is frequently used without the instrumental case. In the dialogue in Unit 12 the instigator of the conversation, Dọr-jé, consistently drops the instrumental case particle when he questions or speaks about Tom, as in ཁྱེད་རང་ དེང་སང་ག་རེ་གནང་གི་ཡོད། ("What are you doing nowadays?" h) and ཁྱེད་རང་བོད་སྐད་ཡག་པོ་མཁྱེན་ གྱི་འདུག། ("You know Tibetan well" h). However, Tom, the responder, switches between not using the instrumental when referring to himself, as when he says ང་དེང་སང་བོད་སྐད་བསླབ་ཀྱི་ ཡོད། ("Nowadays I am studying Tibetan"), and using it, as when he says ངས་དངོས་གནས་ཡག་ པོ་ཤེས་ཀྱི་མེད། ("I really don't know it well").

The following guidelines may be helpful:

- In any tense, the instrumental case is never used with verbs of motion, such as going (འགྲོ་ , ཕྱིནbས་), coming (ཡོང་ , ཕྱིནས་), and arriving (འབྱོར་ , འབྱོར་གནང་ and སླེབ་ , སླེབ་གནང་). Nor is it used with verbs of residing (བསྡད་ , བཞུགས་), needing (དགོས་ , དགོས་གནང་), feeling cold (འཁྱག་ , སྐུ་བསིལ་), and being sick (ན་ , སྐུང་).

- Often the instrumental case is not used with verbs of consumption, such as eating (ཟ་ , མཆོད་), drinking (འཐུང་ , མཆོད་), and licking (ལྡག་ , ལྡག་གནང་), and with verbs of perception such as seeing (མཇལ་), thinking (བསམ་ , དགོངས་), remembering (དྲན་ , དྲན་གནང་), hearing/understanding (གོ་ , གོ་གནང་), and understanding (ཧ་གོ་ , མཁྱེན་).

- For the first person the instrumental case often is dropped unless one wants to stress one's agentive role.

- In third person future tense constructions the instrumental case often is dropped.

For drills with and without the instrumental endings see Unit 12.50-12.60.

DATIVE

The dative case is not mentioned in these fifteen Units. It uses the same endings as the accusative and, technically speaking, marks the recipient of an action only when the recipient obviously benefits from the action as in "The doctor gave medicine *to the patient*." It also makes a purposive verbal construction as in "An axe is needed *to cut* wood. The endings are the same as those for the accusative:

Suffix	Ending
ས་	སུ་
ག་བ་ or extra suffix ད་	ཏུ་
ང་ད་ན་མ་ར་ལ་	དུ་
འ་ or no suffix	རོ་ or ར་

ABLATIVE

The sentence ཁོང་གིས་ཤིང་ཏོག་ཁྲོམ་ནས་གཉེགས་ཀྱི་རེད། means "She (h) will buy fruit from the market." The particle ནས་ ("from") is used in these sentences to mark place of origin or separation, the ablative; the phrase ཁྲོམ་ནས་ means "from the market". Note that Tibetans do *not* say ཁོང་གིས་ཤིང་ཏོག་ཁྲོམ་ལ་གཉེགས་ཀྱི་རེད། ("He will buy fruit *at* the market"). For drills see Unit 9.33-9.48.

GENITIVE

In Unit 12, after asking Tom, "Where do you study?" ག་པར་བསླབ་ཀྱི་ཡོད།, <u>Dor</u>-j é asks ཁྱེད་ རང་གི་དགེ་རྒན་སུ་རེད། ("Who is your teacher?" h). In earlier units we see the particle གི་ used to connect main verbs to auxiliary verbs, but here གི་ is used as a འབྲེལ་སྒྲ་ or "term of relation", the genitive case. The འབྲེལ་སྒྲ་ case can mean many different things. In this example it indicates possession.

Possession is simple ownership, expressed in words that are the equivalent both in sense and in usage to English words such as "my", "your", "her", "our", "their", "Mary's", and so on. In Tibetan, such words are formed by affixing a འབྲེལ་སྒྲ་ to the word indicating the owner. For instance, to ཁྱེད་རང་ ("you" h), <u>Dor</u>-j é adds གི་, forming ཁྱེད་རང་གི་ ("your" h). Replying to <u>Dor</u>-j é's question, Tom adds འི་ to ང་ ("I") making ངའི་ ("my"). These "terms of relation" put ཁྱེད་རང་ and ང་ into relation with the word that follows them, which in both cases is དགེ་རྒན་ ("teacher"). Here, the relationship is one of possession or ownership. Whose དགེ་རྒན་ ("teacher")? ཁྱེད་རང་གི་དགེ་རྒན་ ("Your teacher" h) or ངའི་དགེ་རྒན་ ("My teacher").

As you can see from these examples, the འབྲེལ་སྒྲ་ case connects the owner to the thing owned by being affixed to the word that names the owner and placed before the word that names the thing that is owned. In spoken Tibetan the འབྲེལ་སྒྲ་ takes five different forms. The suffix, secondary suffix, or absence of a suffix terminating the word to which the འབྲེལ་སྒྲ་ is affixed determines which of the five forms of the འབྲེལ་སྒྲ་ is used. Three of these—གི་, ཀྱི་,

and གྱི་ —are quite similar. Here is a chart showing the five འབྲེལ་སྒྲ་ and the suffixes with which they are used.

Suffix	Ending
ད་བ་ས་	གྱི་
ག་ང་	གི་
ན་མ་ར་ལ་	གྱི་
འ་ or no suffix	འི་ or ཡི་ [1]

Suppose you want to say, "Ḍa-shí's teacher". Since བཀྲ་ཤིས་ ends with a ས་ suffix, it takes གྱི་ as its འབྲེལ་སྒྲ་. Hence, "Ḍa-shí's teacher" is བཀྲ་ཤིས་ཀྱི་དགེ་རྒན་. How about "the hospital's food"? Since སྨན་ཁང་ ends with a ང་ suffix, it takes གི་ as its འབྲེལ་སྒྲ་. Thus, "the hospital's food" is སྨན་ཁང་གི་ཁ་ལག. If, at the market, you wanted to comment on the price of the vegetables, you would say ཚལ་གྱི་གོང་ཆེ་ཆུང་ because ཚལ་ ends with a ལ་ suffix and ལ་ takes གྱི་ as its འབྲེལ་སྒྲ་. Still, since the sound of these three འབྲེལ་སྒྲ་ case particles is nearly identical in ordinary conversation, it is suitable just to say "gi". If the word designating the owner ends in འ་ or lacks a suffix, it is put into the genitive case by adding འི་. For instance, ང་ ("I") becomes ངའི་ ("my"); ཁོ་ ("he") becomes ཁོའི་ ("his"); མོ་ ("she") becomes མོའི་ ("her"); ཀུ་ཤུ་ ("apple"), becomes ཀུ་ཤུའི་ ("the apple's" or "of the apple") and so on.

Just as there are many ways in which two things can be related, so the འབྲེལ་སྒྲ་ case can have many meanings. Here we are looking at one of the simplest: a relationship in which one of the two things owns or possesses the other. For drills see Unit 12.67-12.71.

LOCATIVE

In Unit 7 we see the use of ལ་ to mark the destination in a sentence with a verb of motion, as in the sentence ང་ཁྲོམ་ལ་འགྲོ་གི་ཡིན། ("I will go to the market" or "I am going to the market"); in Tibetan, this is the accusative case and not the locative case. This same particle, which functions much like an English preposition (but since it is affixed *after* rather than *before* the word it modifies, it is in fact a *post*position), is also used to mark the place of existence, the locative, as in ཁོང་ཁྲོམ་ལ་འདུག ("She is at the market"). This is the seventh case, བརྟེན་གནས་ཀྱི་སྒྲ་ or "term of dependence and residence", the locative. The endings are the same as those for the accusative:

---

[1] The ending ཡི་ is seldom used in colloquial Tibetan.

Suffix	Ending
ས་	སུ་
ག་བ་or extra suffix ད་	ཏུ་
ང་ད་ན་མ་ར་ལ་	དུ་
འ་ or no suffix	རོ་ or ར་

As with the accusative and dative, the predominant endings are ལ་—since it can be employed with all suffixes—or, when there is no suffix, a ར་ fused with the syllable.

Locative of place. In the final line of the dialogue in Unit 8, ཕ་གིར་འདུག ("[The fruit seller] is over there"), the locative construction is employed to indicate place, but ལ་ is not used because the word to which the location marker is affixed (ཕ་གི་) has no suffix. In such situations, the letter ར་ is used instead of ལ་ and fuses with the syllable to which it is affixed; hence ཕ་གི་ becomes ཕ་གིར་. Such substitution occurs frequently. Later in Unit 8 we see the words ཡ་གི་ and མ་གི་[1] which become ཡ་གིར་ ("up there") and མ་གིར་ ("down there") when indicating a place of existence. Anther common example is འདི་ which, when fused with ར་ as འདིར་, means "here". This is illustrated in the question, ཤིང་ཏོག་ཚོང་མཁན་ག་པར་ འདུག ("Where is the fruit seller?"), and the answer, འདིར་འདུག ("[He or she] is here").

Other important ways of indicating place with the locative case ending ལ་ are:

ནང་ལ་	in, inside
རྒྱབ་ལ་	behind, in back of
མདུན་ལ་	in front of
འཁྲིས་ལ་	near
སྟེང་ལ་	on, on top of
འོག་ལ་	under, beneath, below

In full sentences, each of these particles is preceded by one of the four genitive postpositional particles that basically mean "of" (ཀྱི་, གི་, གྱི་, and འི་), and followed by ལ་ ("at, on, to, etc."). For instance, in reply to the question ཇ་ཁང་ཡག་པོ་ཅིག་ག་པར་འདུག ("Where is there a

---

[1] The word ཡ་གི་ is a pointer meaning "that up there". The word མ་གི་ is a pointer meaning "that down there".

good restaurant?"), one might say ཁྲོམ་གྱི་འགྲིས་ལ་ཡག་པོ་ཅིག་འདུག ("There is a good one near the market"). Similarly, ཟ་ཁང་གི་འགྲིས་ལ་ means "near the restaurant". Here are other examples where objects are placed in relation to other objects:

1 There is a mountain behind the house.	ཁང་པའི་རྒྱབ་ལ་རི་འདུག
2 The mountain is behind the house.	རི་ཁང་པའི་རྒྱབ་ལ་འདུག
3 There is a market near the mountain.	རིའི་འགྲིས་ལ་ཁྲོམ་འདུག
4 The market is near the mountain	ཁྲོམ་རིའི་འགྲིས་ལ་འདུག
5 There is a restaurant near the bank.	དངུལ་ཁང་གི་འགྲིས་ལ་ཟ་ཁང་ཅིག་འདུག
6 A restaurant is near the bank.	ཟ་ཁང་ཅིག་དངུལ་ཁང་གི་འགྲིས་ལ་འདུག
7 There is an inn above the restaurant.	ཟ་ཁང་གི་སྟེང་ལ་གནས་ཚང་འདུག
8 The inn is above the restaurant.	གནས་ཚང་ཟ་ཁང་གི་སྟེང་ལ་འདུག

Since these constructions indicate a place of existence, they never use རེད་. For drills see Unit 9.17-9.22.

Locative of time. The locative case is also used to indicate time, as in the Unit 13 dialogue དེ་རིང་ཆུ་ཚོད་བཅུ་པ་ལ་འཛུག་གི་རེད། ("Today it will meet at ten o'clock"). For drills see Unit 13.34-13.36.

Similarly, the phrase གྱི་སྔོན་ལ་ can be used to indicate when in the past something happened. For instance, a sentence in the dialogue reads ཁོ་བ་གསུམ་གྱི་སྔོན་ལ་ཕེབས་པ་རེད། ("[She] came three months ago" h). The time period, three months, is placed before གྱི་སྔོན་ལ་. Remember that the appropriate form of the genitive case particle must be used. For instance, "five months ago" would be ཁོ་བ་ལྔའི་སྔོན་ལ་. For drills see Unit 14.18-14.21.

Like other languages, Tibetan also uses words denoting specific times, such as དེ་རིང་ ("today"), བདུན་ཕྲེས་མ་ ("next week"), ལོ་ཕྲེས་མ་ ("next year"), and སང་ཉིན་ ("tomorrow") to indicate when an action will be performed. For instance, to say, "I will go home tomorrow", one says, སང་ཉིན་ང་ནང་ལ་འགྲོ་གི་ཡིན། To say, "Next year I will go to India", one says, ལོ་ཕྲེས་མར་ང་རྒྱ་གར་ལ་འགྲོ་གི་ཡིན། As can be seen, in spoken Tibetan some of these use the locative case ending, and some do not. For drills see Unit 12.109-12.110.

Locative of reference. In Unit 14, to ask the name of Tom's friend, Dröl-ma says ཁོང་གི་ མཚན་ལ་ག་རེ་ཞུ་གི་ཡོད་རེད། Grammatically, the particle ལ་ in ཁོང་གི་མཚན་ལ་ is an instance of the བརྟེན་གནས་ཀྱི་སྒྲ་ or "term of dependence and residence", the locative. Among the various meanings of the seventh case, here it carries the sense of reference. A literal translation of the sentence is, "With respect to her name, what does one say?" or, "What does one say for her name?" Tom replies ཁོང་གི་མཚན་ལ་སུའུ་ཛན་ཞུ་གི་ཡོད་རེད། which literally is "With respect to her name, Susan is said," or "For her name, Susan is said." As you can see, the answer preserves the structure of the question, and merely replaces ག་རེ་ ("what") with སུའུ་ཛན་ ("Susan"). For drills see Unit 14.5-14.8.

ADJECTIVES

In the dialogue in Unit 9, Ḍa-shí asks ཟ་ཁང་ཡག་པོ་ཆིག་ག་པར་འདུག། ("Where is a good restaurant?"). In that question, ཡག་པོ་ ("good") qualifies ཟ་ཁང་ ("restaurant"); thus, ཡག་པོ་ serves as an adjective. Tibetan adjectives, like English adjectives, indicate which, what kind of, or how many, but are usually placed after the noun or pronoun that they qualify. (By using the genitive an adjective sometimes can be placed prior to the term it qualifies.)

ARTICLES AND DEMONSTRATIVE ADJECTIVES

Just as English distinguishes "one" from "a" or "an", so Tibetan distinguishes ཟ་ཁང་གཅིག་ ("one restaurant") from ཟ་ཁང་ཅིག་ ("a restaurant"). The only difference in their spelling is the prefix ག་, which does not affect the pronunciation of the root letter ཅ་ but causes the suffix ག་ to be pronounced clearly. However, unlike English, Tibetan does not usually call for an article such as ཅིག་, and thus it is not used anywhere near as frequently as it is in English. It tends to be used when it would be ambiguous whether, for instance, the bare phrase ཟ་ཁང་ ཡག་པོ་ would mean "a good restaurant" or "the good restaurant [you were talking about]"; ཟ་ཁང་ཡག་པོ་ཅིག་, on the other hand, clearly means "a good restaurant".

Also, in Tibetan there is no exact equivalent of "*the* book"; thus དེབ་ alone often suffices. In some contexts དེབ་ is the equivalent of "the book" and in others, "a book". That is to say, Tibetan does not usually call for an article to convey the meaning that "the" does in English, "le" and "la" do in French, "das" and "die" do in German, and so forth. However, Tibetan equivalents for the English demonstrative adjectives "this" (འདི་) and "that" (དེ་) are used frequently. Like other Tibetan adjectives, འདི་ and དེ་ are placed after the nouns that they qualify. So, དེབ་འདི་ means "this book" and དེབ་དེ་, "that book" and, by extension, "the book". Likewise, དེབ་འདི་ཚོ་ means "these books", and དེབ་དེ་ཚོ་ means "those books" and, by extension, "the books".

It is important to note that whereas ཟ་ཁང་ཡག་པོ་ག་པར་འདུག could indicate either "Where is there a good restaurant?" or "Where is the good restaurant?", ཟ་ཁང་ཡག་པོ་དེ་ག་པར་འདུག must mean "Where is that good restaurant?", as you might ask when someone had told you about a good restaurant the day before and you do not know where it is. For drills see Unit 9.5-9.7, 9.11, 9.22-9.25.

In English, "this" can serve either as a pronoun or as an adjective. For instance, in "This is good", "this" is a pronoun, and in "This book is good", "this" is an adjective. Similarly, in Tibetan འདི་ may stand alone as a pronoun or may be used as an adjective. For instance, in འདི་ཡག་པོ་འདུག ("This is good") the word འདི་ is a pronoun, and in དེབ་འདི་ཡག་པོ་འདུག ("This book is good"), the word འདི་ serves as an adjective. The same holds true for དེ་ ("that"): in དེ་ཚོང་ཁང་རེད ("That is a store") the word དེ་ is a pronoun, and in ཚོང་ཁང་དེ་ཆེན་ པོ་རེད ("That store is big") the word དེ་ is an adjective. In the sentence ཚོང་ཁང་འདི་ཆེན་པོ་རེད ("This store is big") ཚོང་ཁང་འདི་ ("this store") is the subject of རེད, and ཆེན་པོ་ ("big") is a predicate adjective. For drills see Unit 9.13.

COMPOUND ADJECTIVES MAKING A NOUN

In Unit 13, after Bethany says that class will meet at ten o'clock, Bé'-ma asks དུས་ཡུན་རིང་ ཐུང་ག་ཚོད་འཆུག་གི་རེད ("How long will [class] meet?"). The word ཡུན་ means "duration" or "period (of time)"; དུས་ means "time". Thus, དུས་ཡུན་ means "period of time". The term རིང་ ཐུང་ is a combination of opposites. The word རིང་པོ་ means "long" and ཐུང་ཐུང་ means "short"; together they mean "length" (literally, "long-short"). The combination of two adjectives opposite in meaning creates an abstract noun that names the quality they share. For instance, མཐོ་པོ་ means "high" and དམན་ means "low"; thus མཐོ་དམན་ means "height". Similarly, ཆེན་པོ་ means "big" and ཆུང་ཆུང་ means "small"; thus ཆེ་ཆུང་ means "size". Again, བཟང་པོ་ means "good" and ངན་པོ་ means "bad"; thus བཟང་ངན་ means "quality". Here is a list of common compounds of this type:

ཚ་གྲང་	temperature (hot-cold)
རིང་ཐུང་	length (long-short)
མཐོ་དམན་	height (high-low)
ཆེ་ཆུང་	size (large-small)
བཟང་ངན་	quality (good-bad)

ཡང་ལྕིད་	weight (light-heavy)
མང་ཉུང་	quantity (many-few)
ཡག་ཉེས་	quality (good-bad)
བདེ་སྡུག་	feeling (pleasure-pain)

For a drill see Unit 13.61.

INTERROGATIVES

INTERROGATIVE PARTICLES

The interrogative particle པས་, as in the question in Unit 4 སྐུ་གཟུགས་བདེ་པོ་ཡིན་པས། ("Are you well?" h), is a common question ending. The response is ང་བདེ་པོ་ཡིན། ("I'm well") or simply བདེ་པོ་ཡིན། ("I'm well"). In responding, one uses the verb pattern that was used in the question but omits the interrogative particle. The third person form uses the pronoun ཁོང་ ("she/he" h) and the third person affirmative form of the verb "to be" རེད་ with the interrogative particle པས་ as in ཁོང་སྐལ་བཟང་ལགས་རེད་པས། ("Is he Gël-sang?" h); the affirmative answer is ལགས་རེད། ཁོང་སྐལ་བཟང་ལགས་རེད། ("Yes, he is Gël-sang" h). Note that in Tibetan, unlike English, one's voice does not rise as much, if at all, at the end of an interrogative sentence.

To repeat: In simple questions such as ཁྱེད་རང་སྐུ་གཟུགས་བདེ་པོ་ཡིན་པས། ("Are you well?" h), ཁྱེད་རང་པད་མ་ལགས་ཡིན་པས། ("Are you Bé'-ma?" h), and ཁོང་འཇིགས་མེད་ལགས་རེད་པས། ("Is he Jík-mé'?" h), the interrogative is marked by the particle པས་, and in answering them one merely omits the particle པས་ and mirrors the verb that was used in the question, either in the affirmative or the negative. Thus, to the question ཁྱེད་རང་སྐུ་གཟུགས་བདེ་པོ་ཡིན་པས། ("Are you well?" h) you might answer ལགས་བདེ་པོ་ཡིན། ("Yes, I am well"), and to the question ཁྱེད་རང་པད་མ་ལགས་ཡིན་པས། ("Are you Bé'-ma?" h) you might answer ལགས་མིན། པད་མ་མིན། ("No, I'm not Bé'-ma"). Likewise, to the question ཁོང་འཇིགས་མེད་ལགས་རེད་པས། ("Is he Jík-mé'?" h) you might answer ལགས་རེད། ཁོང་འཇིགས་མེད་ལགས་རེད། ("Yes, he is Jík-mé'" h) or ལགས་མ་རེད། ཁོང་འཇིགས་མེད་ལགས་མ་རེད། ("No, he is not Jík-mé'" h). For drills, see Unit 4.8-4.23.

With འདུག the interrogative particle is གས་ as in གློག་བརྙན་ཁང་པ་གིར་འདུག་གས། ("Is the cinema over there?"); for drills see Unit 7.31, etc. With ཡོང་ the interrogative particle is ངས་

as in ཁོང་གིས་ཕྱག་ལས་གནང་སོང་ངས། ("Did he/she work?" or "Was he/she working?" h); for drills see Unit 14.15, etc.

SHORTENED FORMS OMITTING THE SUBJECT

When asking a second person question such as ཁྱེད་རང་པད་མ་ལགས་ཡིན་པས། ("Are you B̄é'-ma?" h), one uses the form of the verb that will be used in the answer. Thus, one might just as clearly have said པད་མ་ལགས་ཡིན་པས། ("Are you B̄é'-ma?" h), omitting the pronoun ཁྱེད་རང་ ("you" h) which is obvious. In practice, Tibetans tend to use the shortened form more than the full form. In answer to the question, ཁྱེད་རང་པད་མ་ལགས་ཡིན་པས། ("Are you B̄é'-ma?" h), one might say པད་མ་ཡིན། ("[I] am B̄é'-ma") instead of ང་པད་མ་ཡིན། ("I am B̄é'-ma"), omitting the pronoun ང་ ("I") without any loss of clarity. For the third person, in answer to the question ཁོང་སྐལ་བཟང་ལགས་རེད་པས། ("Is she Ḡël-sang?" h), rather than saying ལགས་རེད། ཁོང་སྐལ་བཟང་ལགས་རེད། ("Yes, she is Ḡël-sang" h), one says ལགས་རེད། སྐལ་བཟང་ལགས་རེད། ("Yes, she is Ḡël-sang" h), omitting the personal pronoun ཁོང་ ("she/he" h). For drills see Unit 4.7, 4.9, 4.11, 4.13, 4.16, 4.18, 4.20, 4.22.

THE ABBREVIATED ANSWER ལགས་ཡིན།

In responding to questions, Tibetans often give an initial abbreviated answer beginning with the particle ལགས་ (which here means "Yes" or perhaps simply "I have heard you") with the affirmative or negative verb ending used in the question. Thus, in answering the question ཁྱེད་རང་བཀྲ་ཤིས་ལགས་ཡིན་པས། ("Are you D̤a-s̄hí?" h), one might politely say ལགས་ཡིན། ང་བཀྲ་ཤིས་ཡིན། ("Yes, I am D̤a-s̄hí") or, in the negative, ལགས་མིན། ང་བཀྲ་ཤིས་མིན། ("No, I am not D̤a-s̄hí"). For the third person use ལགས་རེད། and ལགས་མ་རེད།. For drills see Unit 4.8-4.22.

WHO?

Unit 5 begins working with questions constructed using the interrogative pronouns སུ་ ("who"). Second person questions with an interrogative pronoun end with the particle པ་. For instance, "Who are you?" (h) is ཁྱེད་རང་སུ་ཡིན་པ།. Third person questions with an interrogative pronoun have no special particle ending. For instance, "Who is she/he?" (h) is ཁོང་སུ་རེད།. Study the following chart to understand the structure:

ཁྱེད་རང་སུ་ཡིན་པ།	Who are you?
བཀྲ་ཤིས་ཚེ་རིང་ཡིན།	[I] am D̤a-s̄hí Tshé-ríng.

ཁོང་སུ་རེད།   Who is she?

བསོད་ནམས་ལགས་རེད།   [She] is Sö'-nam.

ཁོང་སུ་རེད།   Who is he?

བློ་བཟང་དོན་གྲུབ་ལགས་རེད།   [He] is Lo-sang Tön-dup.

For drills see Unit 5.5-5.6.

WHOSE?

The interrogative pronoun སུ་ ("who") is combined with the genitive particle འི་ to create the interrogative possessive pronoun སུའི་ ("whose"), as in the sentence ཕྱག་དངུལ་འདི་སུའི་རེད། ("Whose money is this?" h). For drills see Unit 12.70-12.71.

WHAT?

In the Unit 7 dialogue the interrogative particle ག་རེ་ ("what") is used when Tön-dup asks Da-shí what he will buy at the market ཁྱེད་རང་ག་རེ་གཉེགས་ཀྱི་ཡིན་པ། ("What will you buy?" h).

WHERE?

In the Unit 6 dialogue the interrogative particle ག་པར་ ("where") is used when Bé'-ma asks Gël-sang where he is going ག་པར་ཕེབས་ཀ། ("Where are you going?"). For drills see Unit 9.5-9.6, 9.30, 9.32, 10.43-10.44.

FROM WHERE?

Tibetans commonly ask ག་ནས་ཡིན་པ། ("Where are you from?"). The word ག་ནས་ is an interrogative particle that means "from where" and ཡིན་པ་ means "are" (used predominantly for the first person). One responds by saying, for instance, ཨ་མེ་རི་ག་ནས་ཡིན། ("I am from America"). For drills see Unit 9.33-9.34.

WHEN?

In the Unit 13 dialogue the interrogative particle ག་དུས་ ("when") is used to ask when class will meet དེ་རིང་འཛིན་གྲྭ་ག་དུས་འཆུག་གི་རེད། ("When will class meet today?"). For drills see Unit 9.27-29, 11.34, 12.109-12.110, 13.56, 13.58-13.59.

HOW?

In Unit 11 the interrogative particle ག་འདྲས་ ("how") is introduced as in གསོལ་ཇ་མང་ར་མོ་ག

འདྲས་འདུག ("How is the sweet tea?" h). There verb རེད་ tends not to be used with ག་འདྲས་.
For drills see Unit11.22-11.31.

HOW MANY?

The words ག་ཚོད་ and ག་ཚད་ mean "how many?" or "how much?". Questions with "how many?" or "how much?" can be asked using any appropriate variant of the verb "to be". For drills see Unit 10.40-10.43. For drills about time see Unit 13.54-13.55, 13.57.

In Unit 13, after Bethany says that class will meet at ten o'clock, Bé'-ma asks དུས་ཡུན་རིང་ ཐུང་ག་ཚོད་འཆུག་གི་རེད ("How long will [class] meet?"). The word ཡུན་ means "duration" or "period (of time)"; དུས་ means "time". Thus, དུས་ཡུན་ means "period of time". The term རིང་ ཐུང་ is a combination of opposites. The word རིང་པོ་ means "long" and ཐུང་ཐུང་ means "short"; together they mean "length" (literally, "long-short"). The combination of two adjectives opposite in meaning creates an abstract noun that names the quality they share. For a drill see Unit 13.61.

WHAT KINDS? HOW MANY PLACES?

In the Unit 10 dialogue Tön-dup asks ཞལ་ལག་ག་རེ་ག་རེ་ཡོད་རེད ("What kinds of food are there?" h). Notice the doubling of ག་རེ་ into ག་རེ་ག་རེ་. Such doubling of interrogative particles is common and indicates multiplicity. Here, ག་རེ་ག་རེ་ expresses the notion that the restaurant serves a variety of dishes and asks for a list of them. If Tön-dup and Da-shí were discussing a trip that their friend Tsé-ríng was about to take, one of them might say ཁོང་ག་ པར་ག་པར་ཕེབས་ཀྱི་རེད, meaning "How many places will she go to?" (h). By doubling the interrogative ག་པར་ the speaker is saying, "I'm assuming that she will go to a variety of places. Would you list them?" For drills see Unit 10.25-10.30.

CHOICES

In Unit 11, after agreeing to Sö'-nam's suggestion that they drink tea, Dé-gyí' asks གསོལ་ཇ་ ག་རེ་མཆོད་ཀ། གསོལ་ཇ་མངར་མོ་མཆོད་ཀ། ཀོ་ཕེ་མཆོད་ཀ། ("What 'tea' will you drink? Will you drink sweet tea? Or coffee?" h). This exchange demonstrates how one suggests or inquires about alternative possibilities. The construction is simple: object + verb + ཀ + object + verb + ཀ. In other words, one states each alternative plainly and concludes each one with a slightly lengthened ཀ. Thus, གསོལ་ཇ་མངར་མོ་མཆོད་ཀ། ཀོ་ཕེ་མཆོད་ཀ། ("Will you drink sweet tea? Or coffee?" h). To ask, "Will you go to Hla-ša or to Dé-gé (h)," one would say ལྷ་སར་ ཕེབས་ཀ། སྡེ་དགེར་ཕེབས་ཀ།. For drills see Unit 11.15-11.21.

VERBS

THE VERB "TO BE"

An important point raised in Unit 7 is the different usages of འདུག and རེད to express being. In English, "She is over there" says something about where she exists. "She is an American" says something about who she is. The verb "is" functions differently in these statements. In Tibetan, different verbs are used to indicate something about *where* a person or object exists and to indicate *who* or *what* a person or object is. The verb འདུག is used in the sentence ཤིང་ཏོག་ཚོང་མཁན་པ་གྱེར་འདུག ("The fruit seller is over there") because one is saying *where* the seller is. The verb རེད is used in the sentence ཁོང་ཨ་མེ་རི་ཀ་རེད ("She is an American") because one is declaring *who* she is. Thus, འདུག is used for location, but རེད is not. For drills see Unit 7.30-7.31.

The situation is complicated by the fact that both འདུག and རེད are also used as linking verbs for predicate adjectives (and sometimes even for predicate nouns modified by adjectives). It is helpful to keep in mind that རེད is used as a linking verb often in situations of objective certainty, such as ཁང་པ་འདི་དཀར་པོ་རེད ("This house is white"), whereas འདུག is used as a linking verb for more subjective opinions, such as ཁང་པ་འདི་སྐྱིད་པོ་འདུག ("This house is comfortable") and ཟ་ཁང་འདི་སྡུག་ཆག་ཅིག་འདུག ("This restaurant is awful"), or when you have checked and found a situation to be so. Thus, although both རེད and འདུག are used to connect a subject and a predicate adjective, the two are not strictly interchangeable. There is continuity between questions and answers, for questions asked with འདུག are answered with འདུག and questions asked with རེད are answered with རེད. For drills see Unit 9.8-9.25, 10.48, 11.32-11.33.

The Unit 10 dialogue introduces ཡོད་རེད which, like འདུག, can both indicate existence in a place and as a linking verb connecting a subject with a predicate adjective. Although འདུག and ཡོད་རེད are often used somewhat interchangeably, they sometimes indicate different meanings. Thus, sometimes བོད་ལ་གཡག་མང་པོ་འདུག can indicate that one knows from experience that there are many yaks in Tibet. Conversely, བོད་ལ་གཡག་མང་པོ་ཡོད་རེད can indicate that one merely knows *of* this. For this reason, statements about the weather when one has direct experience of it are made with འདུག. Still, it is important to remember that in other situations this distinction is not strict and that the two expressions are sometimes used interchangeably. For drills see Unit 10.5-10.24, 10.47, 11.22-11.31.

Similarly, sometimes རྒྱ་གར་དྲོས་གནས་ཚ་པོ་འདུག ("India is really hot") can indicate that one knows from experience that India is hot. Conversely, རྒྱ་གར་དྲོས་གནས་ཚ་པོ་རེད and རྒྱ

གར་དངོས་གནས་ཆ་པོ་ཡོད་རེད། can indicate that one merely knows *of* this. However, it is important to remember that this distinction is not strict and that the expressions are sometimes used interchangeably. For drills see Unit 10.14-10.18.

In Unit 11 Dé-ḡyí says about the tea གྲང་མོ་རེད། ཆ་པོ་མི་འདུག ("[The tea] is cold; it isn't hot"). Notice the shift from རེད to འདུག. Sö'-nam uses འདུག to say that the tea is not hot (ཆ་པོ་མི་འདུག) and རེད to say that it is cold (གྲང་མོ་རེད།). She also could have said ཆ་པོ་མི་འདུག གྲང་མོ་འདུག or ཆ་པོ་མ་རེད། གྲང་མོ་རེད། or ཆ་པོ་ཡོད་མ་རེད། གྲང་མོ་ཡོད་རེད།. Thus, this is an example of the general interchangeability of རེད, འདུག, and ཡོད་རེད; still, the boundaries of their interchangeability need to be known. Sometimes when a difference is made, ཡོད་རེད is used to express a general observation; thus ཆ་པོ་ཡོད་མ་རེད། could indicate that the tea in this restaurant generally is not hot. The following table explains, in general terms, the usage of the verb "to be" for all three persons, beginning with the third.

THIRD PERSON

Type 1. noun + noun + verb "to be"

རེད exclusively

ཁོང་བོད་པ་རེད། ("She is a Tibetan" h).

NEVER say ཁོང་བོད་པ་འདུག or ཁོང་བོད་པ་ཡོད་རེད། or ཁོང་བོད་པ་ཡོད། [1]

Type 2. noun + adjective + verb "to be"

རེད, འདུག, and ཡོད་རེད basically are used interchangeably

ཁོང་ཕྱུག་པོ་རེད།, ཁོང་ཕྱུག་པོ་འདུག, and ཁོང་ཕྱུག་པོ་ཡོད་རེད། ("He is rich" h). [2]

Type 3. noun + noun + adjective + verb "to be"

རེད, འདུག, and ཡོད་རེད basically are used interchangeably

ཁོང་མི་ཕྱུག་པོ་རེད།, ཁོང་མི་ཕྱུག་པོ་འདུག, and ཁོང་མི་ཕྱུག་པོ་ཡོད་རེད། ("He is a rich man" h). [3]

Notice that here the predicate is treated like a predicate adjective (type 2) and

---

[1] Although ཁོང་བོད་པ་ཡིན། could not be used as a complete clause, it can be used in such phrases as ཁོང་བོད་པ་ཡིན་ཙང་ ("Because she is a Tibetan...") and ཁོང་བོད་པ་ཡིན་པ་འདྲ། ("She seems to be Tibetan").

[2] Although ཁོང་ཕྱུག་པོ་ཡིན། could not be used as a complete clause, it can be used in such phrases as ཁོང་ཕྱུག་པོ་ཡིན་ཙང་ ("Because he is rich...") and ཁོང་ཕྱུག་པོ་ཡིན་པ་འདྲ། ("He seems to be rich").

[3] Although ཁོང་མི་ཕྱུག་པོ་ཡིན། could not be used as a complete clause, it can be used in such phrases as ཁོང་མི་ཕྱུག་པོ་ཡིན་ཙང་ ("Because he is a rich person...") and ཁོང་མི་ཕྱུག་པོ་ཡིན་པ་འདྲ། ("He seems to be a rich person").

not like a predicate nominative (type 1) as it would be in English. This is why འདུག and ཡོད་རེད་ can be used. Nevertheless, some Central Tibetans do not use these two.

Type 4. noun + location + verb "to be"

འདུག and ཡོད་རེད་ basically are used interchangeably

ཁོང་ཕ་གིར་འདུག and ཁོང་ཕ་གིར་ཡོད་རེད། ("She is over there" h).

NEVER say ཁོང་ཕ་གིར་ཡིན། or ཁོང་ཕ་གིར་རེད། [1]

Type 5. possessive statements

འདུག and ཡོད་རེད་ basically are used interchangeably

ཁོང་ལ་ཕྱུག་དངུལ་མང་པོ་འདུག and ཁོང་ལ་ཕྱུག་དངུལ་མང་པོ་ཡོད་རེད། ("He has a lot of money" h).

NEVER say ཁོང་ལ་ཕྱུག་དངུལ་མང་པོ་རེད། or ཁོང་ལ་ཕྱུག་དངུལ་མང་པོ་ཡིན།

Comment: Note that འདུག and ཡོད་རེད་ are used both to connect subject and predicate and for place of existence like the English "am", "are", and "is" as for instance in "He is rich" and "He is over there." The copulative verb རེད་, however, is used only to connect subject and predicate, as in "He is rich"; it is never used for place of existence.

When a difference is made between འདུག, རེད་, and ཡོད་རེད་ as, for instance, between ཁོང་ཕྱུག་པོ་འདུག on the one hand and ཁོང་ཕྱུག་པོ་རེད། and ཁོང་ཕྱུག་པོ་ཡོད་རེད། on the other hand, the former often indicates personal verification whereas the latter two are more general statements. The situation is complicated by the fact that purely objective statements are sometimes made with རེད་ as in ཁོང་པ་དེ་དམར་པོ་རེད། ("That house is red"), whereas subjective and judgmental statements are sometimes made with འདུག, as in ཞལ་ལག་འདི་སྟོ་པོ་འདུག ("This food is tasty" h).

SECOND PERSON
Type 1. noun + noun + verb "to be"

རེད་ exclusively

ཁྱེད་རང་བོད་པ་རེད། ("You are a Tibetan" h).

---

[1] Although ཁོང་ཕ་གིར་ཡོད། could not be used as a complete clause, it can be used in such phrases as ཁོང་ཕ་གིར་ཡོད་ཙང་ ("Because he is over there...") and ཁོང་ཕ་གིར་ཡོད་པ་འདྲ། ("He seems to be over there").

NEVER say ཁྱེད་རང་བོད་པ་འདུག or ཁྱེད་རང་བོད་པ་ཡོད་རེད or ཁྱེད་རང་བོད་པ་ཡོད། [1]

Type 2. noun + adjective + verb "to be"

རེད་, འདུག, and ཡོད་རེད་ basically are used interchangeably

ཁྱེད་རང་ཕྱུག་པོ་རེད།, ཁྱེད་རང་ཕྱུག་པོ་འདུག, and ཁྱེད་རང་ཕྱུག་པོ་ཡོད་རེད། ("You are rich" h)[2]

Second person interrogatives employ ཨིན་, རེད་, and ཡོད་རེད་

ཁྱེད་རང་ཕྱུག་པོ་ཨིན་པས, ཁྱེད་རང་ཕྱུག་པོ་རེད་པས, and ཁྱེད་རང་ཕྱུག་པོ་ཡོད་རེད་པས ("Are you rich?" h)

Exceptional usage: ཁྱེད་རང་ཕྱུག་པོ་ཡོད་པས. ("Are you rich?" h)

NEVER say ཁྱེད་རང་ཕྱུག་པོ་འདུག་གས།

Type 3. noun + noun + adjective + verb "to be"

རེད་, འདུག, and ཡོད་རེད་ basically are used interchangeably

ཁྱེད་རང་མི་ཕྱུག་པོ་རེད།, ཁྱེད་རང་མི་ཕྱུག་པོ་འདུག, and ཁྱེད་རང་མི་ཕྱུག་པོ་ཡོད་རེད། ("You are a rich man" h).[3]

> Notice that here the predicate is treated like a predicate adjective (type 2) and not like a predicate nominative (type 1) as it would be in English. This is why འདུག and ཡོད་རེད་ can be used. Nevertheless, some Central Tibetans do not use these two.

Second person interrogatives also employ ཨིན།

ཁྱེད་རང་མི་ཕྱུག་པོ་ཨིན་པས, ཁྱེད་རང་མི་ཕྱུག་པོ་རེད་པས, and ཁྱེད་རང་མི་ཕྱུག་པོ་ཡོད་རེད་པས། ("Are you a rich man?" h)

Exceptional usage: ཁྱེད་རང་མི་ཕྱུག་པོ་ཡོད་པས། ("Are you a rich man?" h)

NEVER say ཁྱེད་རང་མི་ཕྱུག་པོ་འདུག་གས།

---

[1] Although ཁྱེད་རང་བོད་པ་ཨིན། could not be used as a complete clause, it can be used in such phrases as ཁྱེད་རང་བོད་པ་ཨིན་ཙང་ ("Because you are a Tibetan…") and ཁྱེད་རང་བོད་པ་ཨིན་པ་འདྲ། ("You seem to be a Tibetan").

[2] Although ཁྱེད་རང་ཕྱུག་པོ་ཨིན། could not be used as a complete clause, it can be used in such phrases as ཁྱེད་རང་ཕྱུག་པོ་ཨིན་ཙང་ ("Because you are rich…") and ཁྱེད་རང་ཕྱུག་པོ་ཨིན་པ་འདྲ། ("You seem to be rich").

[3] Although ཁྱེད་རང་མི་ཕྱུག་པོ་ཨིན། could not be used as a complete clause, it can be used in such phrases as ཁྱེད་རང་མི་ཕྱུག་པོ་ཨིན་ཙང་ ("Because you are a rich person…") and ཁྱེད་རང་མི་ཕྱུག་པོ་ཨིན་པ་འདྲ། ("You seem to be a rich person").

Type 4. noun + location + verb "to be"

འདུག and ཡོད་རེད་ basically are used interchangeably

ཁྱེད་རང་ཕ་གིར་འདུག and ཁྱེད་རང་ཕ་གིར་ཡོད་རེད། ("You are over there" h).[1]

NEVER say ཁྱེད་རང་ཕ་གིར་ཡིན། or ཁྱེད་རང་ཕ་གིར་རེད།

Second person interrogatives use ཡོད་པས་ and ཡོད་རེད་པས་

ཁྱེད་རང་ཕ་གིར་ཡོད་པས། and ཁྱེད་རང་ཕ་གིར་ཡོད་རེད་པས། ("Are you over there?" h).

Type 5. possessive statements

འདུག and ཡོད་རེད་ basically are used interchangeably

ཁྱེད་རང་ལ་སྤྱག་དངུལ་མང་པོ་འདུག and ཁྱེད་རང་ལ་སྤྱག་དངུལ་མང་པོ་ཡོད་རེད། ("You have a lot of money" h).

NEVER say ཁྱེད་རང་ལ་སྤྱག་དངུལ་མང་པོ་རེད། or ཁྱེད་རང་ལ་སྤྱག་དངུལ་མང་པོ་ཡིན།

Comment: When a difference is made between འདུག , རེད་ and ཡོད་རེད་ as, for instance, between ཁྱེད་རང་སྤྱག་པོ་འདུག on the one hand and ཁྱེད་རང་སྤྱག་པོ་རེད། and ཁྱེད་རང་སྤྱག་པོ་ཡོད་རེད། on the other hand, the former often indicates personal verification whereas the latter are more general statements.

FIRST PERSON

Type 1. noun + noun + verb "to be"

ཡིན་ basically
ང་ཨ་མེ་རི་ཀ་ཡིན། ("I am an American").

རེད་ also can be used
ང་ཨ་མེ་རི་ཀ་རེད། ("I am an American").

NEVER say ང་ཨ་མེ་རི་ཀ་འདུག or ང་ཨ་མེ་རི་ཀ་ཡོད་རེད། or ང་ཨ་མེ་རི་ཀ་ཡོད།

Type 2. noun + adjective + verb "to be"

ཡིན་ basically
ང་དྲང་པོ་ཡིན། ("I am honest").

---

[1] Although ཁྱེད་རང་ཕ་གིར་ཡོད། could not be used as a complete clause, it can be used in such phrases as ཁྱེད་རང་ཕ་གིར་ཡོད་ཙང་ ("Because you are over there...") and ཁྱེད་རང་ཕ་གིར་ཡོད་པའདྲ། ("You seem to be over there").

རེད་ and ཡོད་རེད་ also can be used

ང་དྲང་པོ་རེད། and ང་དྲང་པོ་ཡོད་རེད། ("I am honest").

Exceptional usage: ང་དྲང་པོ་ཡོད། ("I exist [as] honest").

NEVER say ང་དྲང་པོ་འདུག།

Type 3. noun + noun + adjective + verb "to be"

ཡིན་ basically

ང་མི་དྲང་པོ་ཡིན། ("I am an honest person").

རེད་ and ཡོད་རེད་ also can be used

ང་མི་དྲང་པོ་རེད། and ང་མི་དྲང་པོ་ཡོད་རེད། ("I am an honest person").

> Notice that here the predicate is treated like a predicate adjective (type 2) and not like a predicate nominative (type 1) as it would be in English. This is why ཡོད་རེད་ can be used.

Exceptional usage: ང་མི་དྲང་པོ་ཡོད། ("I exist [as] as an honest person").

NEVER say ང་མི་དྲང་པོ་འདུག།

Type 4. noun + location + verb "to be"

ཡོད་ basically

ང་གྲོང་ཁྱེར་ལ་ཡོད། ("I am in the city").

ཡོད་རེད་ is also used

ང་གྲོང་ཁྱེར་ལ་ཡོད་རེད། ("I am in the city").

NEVER say ང་གྲོང་ཁྱེར་ལ་ཡིན། or ང་གྲོང་ཁྱེར་ལ་རེད། or ང་གྲོང་ཁྱེར་ལ་འདུག།

Type 5. possessive statements

ཡོད་ basically

ང་ལ་དངུལ་མང་པོ་ཡོད། ("I have a lot of money").

ཡོད་རེད་ is also used

ང་ལ་དངུལ་མང་པོ་ཡོད་རེད། ("I have a lot of money").

Exceptional usage: ང་ལ་དངུལ་མང་པོ་འདུག། ("I do have a lot of money"). This could be said in a situation when you thought you did not have much money with you, but you searched through your pockets and discovered that indeed you do have a lot of money. Thus, if someone knew that you had made a search, that person could ask you ཁྱེད་རང་ལ་ཕྱག་དངུལ་མང་པོ་འདུག་གས།.

NEVER say ང་ལ་དངུལ་མང་པོ་རེད། or ང་ལ་དངུལ་མང་པོ་ཡིན།

Guidelines:

1. འདུག is never used as a verb "to be" and almost never to indicate place of existence **for the first person** and, by extension, **for second person interrogative.**[1]
2. རེད and ཡིན are **never** used to indicate place of existence.
3. ཡོད་རེད is used to connect subject and predicate and to indicate place of existence **for all three persons.**

BASIC VERB "TO BE"

The constructions indicated just above are now given in chart form:

BASIC VERB "TO BE" AFFIRMATIVE DECLARATIVE

Basic Verb "To Be" Affirmative Declarative: noun + noun + verb "to be"			
Singular		*Plural*	
ང་བོད་པ་ཡིན།	I am a Tibetan	ང་ཚོ་བོད་པ་ཡིན།	We are Tibetans
ཁྱེད་རང་བོད་པ་རེད།	You are a Tibetan (h)	ཁྱེད་རང་ཚོ་བོད་པ་རེད།	You are Tibetans (h)
ཁོང་བོད་པ་རེད།	She/he is a Tibetan (h)	ཁོང་ཚོ་བོད་པ་རེད།	They (m/f) are Tibetans (h)

For all verb charts use the other appropriate pronouns as indicated above in the section on pronouns.

---

[1] An exception to this rule can occur in a circumstance such as when you thought you had no money with you but a thorough search turns up some money; at that point you could say ངར་དངུལ་འདུག ("I *do* have money"); thus, if someone knew that you had made a search, that person could ask you ཁྱེད་རང་ལ་ཕྱག་དངུལ་མང་པོ་འདུག་གས།. As will be seen in the next unit, གི་འདུག is sometimes used as an auxiliary verb ending (*not* as a form of the verb "to be") for certain first person verbs.

Basic Verb "To Be" Affirmative Declarative: noun + adjective + verb "to be"			
Singular		*Plural*	
ང་དྲང་པོ་ཡིན།	I am honest[1]	ང་ཚོ་དྲང་པོ་ཡིན།	We are honest
ཁྱེད་རང་དྲང་པོ་རེད། ཁྱེད་རང་དྲང་པོ་འདུག ཁྱེད་རང་དྲང་པོ་ཡོད་རེད།	You are honest (h)	ཁྱེད་རང་ཚོ་དྲང་པོ་རེད། ཁྱེད་རང་ཚོ་དྲང་པོ་འདུག ཁྱེད་རང་ཚོ་དྲང་པོ་ཡོད་ རེད།	You are honest (h)
ཁོང་དྲང་པོ་རེད། ཁོང་དྲང་པོ་འདུག ཁོང་དྲང་པོ་ཡོད་རེད།	She/he is honest (h)	ཁོང་ཚོ་དྲང་པོ་རེད། ཁོང་ཚོ་དྲང་པོ་འདུག ཁོང་ཚོ་དྲང་པོ་ཡོད་རེད།	They (m/f) are honest (h)

Basic Verb "To Be" Affirmative Declarative: noun + noun + adjective + verb "to be"			
Singular		*Plural*	
ང་མི་དྲང་པོ་ཡིན།	I am an honest person	ང་ཚོ་མི་དྲང་པོ་ཡིན།	We are honest people
ཁྱེད་རང་མི་དྲང་པོ་རེད། ཁྱེད་རང་མི་དྲང་པོ་འདུག ཁྱེད་རང་མི་དྲང་པོ་ཡོད་ རེད།	You are an honest person (h)	ཁྱེད་རང་ཚོ་མི་དྲང་པོ་རེད། ཁྱེད་རང་ཚོ་མི་དྲང་པོ་ འདུག ཁྱེད་རང་ཚོ་མི་དྲང་པོ་ ཡོད་རེད།	You are honest people (h)
ཁོང་མི་དྲང་པོ་རེད། ཁོང་མི་དྲང་པོ་འདུག ཁོང་མི་དྲང་པོ་ཡོད་རེད།	She/he is an honest person (h)	ཁོང་ཚོ་མི་དྲང་པོ་རེད། ཁོང་ཚོ་མི་དྲང་པོ་འདུག ཁོང་ཚོ་མི་དྲང་པོ་ཡོད་ རེད།	They (m/f) are honest people (h)

---

[1] The phrase ང་དྲང་པོ་ཡིན། also can mean "I am being honest" in the sense of "I am telling the truth." The same applies to both questions and answers in all persons.

Basic Verb "To Be" Affirmative Declarative: noun + location + verb "to be"			
Singular		*Plural*	
ང་གྲོང་ཁྱེར་ལ་ཡོད།	I am in the city	ང་ཚོ་གྲོང་ཁྱེར་ལ་ཡོད།	We are in the city
ཁྱེད་རང་ཕ་གིར་འདུག ཁྱེད་རང་ཕ་གིར་ཡོད་རེད།	You are over there (h)	ཁྱེད་རང་ཚོ་ཕ་གིར་འདུག ཁྱེད་རང་ཚོ་ཕ་གིར་ཡོད་ རེད།	You are over there (h)
ཁོང་ཕ་གིར་འདུག ཁོང་ཕ་གིར་ཡོད་རེད།	She/he is over there (h)	ཁོང་ཚོ་ཕ་གིར་འདུག ཁོང་ཚོ་ཕ་གིར་ཡོད་རེད།	They (m/f) are over there (h)

Basic Verb "To Be" Affirmative Declarative: Possessive			
Singular		*Plural*	
ང་ལ་ཕྱུག་དངུལ་མང་པོ་ ཡོད།[1]	I have a lot of money	ང་ཚོ་ལ་ཕྱུག་དངུལ་མང་ པོ་ཡོད།	We have a lot of money
ཁྱེད་རང་ལ་ཕྱུག་དངུལ་ མང་པོ་འདུག ཁྱེད་རང་ལ་ཕྱུག་དངུལ་ མང་པོ་ཡོད་རེད།	You have a lot of money (h)	ཁྱེད་རང་ཚོ་ལ་ཕྱུག་དངུལ་ མང་པོ་འདུག ཁྱེད་རང་ཚོ་ལ་ཕྱུག་དངུལ་ མང་པོ་ཡོད་རེད།	You have a lot of money (h)
ཁོང་ལ་ཕྱུག་དངུལ་མང་པོ་ འདུག ཁོང་ལ་ཕྱུག་དངུལ་མང་པོ་ ཡོད་རེད།	She/he has a lot of money (h)	ཁོང་ཚོ་ལ་ཕྱུག་དངུལ་མང་ པོ་འདུག ཁོང་ཚོ་ལ་ཕྱུག་དངུལ་མང་ པོ་ཡོད་རེད།	They (m/f) have a lot of money (h)

---

[1] In words that do not have a suffix, the particle ར་ can be used in place of ལ་, in which case it is fused directly to the word. Thus, ང་ལ་དངུལ་མང་པོ་ཡོད། ("I have a lot of money") can also be said ངར་དངུལ་མང་པོ་ཡོད། Similarly, ང་ཚོར་ can be said for ང་ཚོ་ལ་, ཁྱེད་རང་ཚོར་ for ཁྱེད་རང་ཚོ་ལ་, ཁོང་ཚོར་ for ཁོང་ཚོ་ལ་, and so forth.

BASIC VERB "TO BE" NEGATIVE DECLARATIVE

Basic Verb "To Be" Negative Declarative: noun + noun + verb "to be"			
Singular		*Plural*	
ང་བོད་པ་མེན།	I am not a Tibetan	ང་ཚོ་བོད་པ་མེན།	We are not Tibetans
ཁྱེད་རང་བོད་པ་མ་རེད།	You are not a Tibetan (h)	ཁྱེད་རང་ཚོ་བོད་པ་མ་རེད།	You are not Tibetans (h)
ཁོང་བོད་པ་མ་རེད།	She/he is not a Tibetan (h)	ཁོང་ཚོ་བོད་པ་མ་རེད།	They (m/f) are not Tibetans (h)

Basic Verb "To Be" Negative Declarative: noun + adjective + verb "to be"			
Singular		*Plural*	
ང་དྲང་པོ་མེན།	I am not honest	ང་ཚོ་དྲང་པོ་མེན།	We are not honest
ཁྱེད་རང་དྲང་པོ་མ་རེད། ཁྱེད་རང་དྲང་པོ་མི་འདུག ཁྱེད་རང་དྲང་པོ་ཡོད་མ་རེད།	You are not honest (h)	ཁྱེད་རང་ཚོ་དྲང་པོ་མ་རེད། ཁྱེད་རང་ཚོ་དྲང་པོ་མི་འདུག ཁྱེད་རང་ཚོ་དྲང་པོ་ཡོད་མ་རེད།	You are not honest (h)
ཁོང་དྲང་པོ་མ་རེད། ཁོང་དྲང་པོ་མི་འདུག ཁོང་དྲང་པོ་ཡོད་མ་རེད།	She/he is not honest (h)	ཁོང་ཚོ་དྲང་པོ་མ་རེད། ཁོང་ཚོ་དྲང་པོ་མི་འདུག ཁོང་ཚོ་དྲང་པོ་ཡོད་མ་རེད།	They (m/f) are not honest (h)

Basic Verb "To Be" Negative Declarative: noun + noun + adjective + verb "to be"			
Singular		*Plural*	
ང་མི་དྲང་པོ་མེན།	I am not an honest person	ང་ཚོ་མི་དྲང་པོ་མེན།	We are not honest people
ཁྱེད་རང་མི་དྲང་པོ་མ་རེད། ཁྱེད་རང་མི་དྲང་པོ་མི་འདུག ཁྱེད་རང་མི་དྲང་པོ་ཡོད་མ་རེད།	You are not an honest person (h)	ཁྱེད་རང་ཚོ་མི་དྲང་པོ་མ་རེད། ཁྱེད་རང་ཚོ་མི་དྲང་པོ་མི་འདུག ཁྱེད་རང་ཚོ་མི་དྲང་པོ་ཡོད་མ་རེད།	You are not honest people (h)
ཁོང་མི་དྲང་པོ་མ་རེད། ཁོང་མི་དྲང་པོ་མི་འདུག ཁོང་མི་དྲང་པོ་ཡོད་མ་རེད།	She/he is not an honest person (h)	ཁོང་ཚོ་མི་དྲང་པོ་མ་རེད། ཁོང་ཚོ་མི་དྲང་པོ་མི་འདུག ཁོང་ཚོ་མི་དྲང་པོ་ཡོད་མ་རེད།	They (m/f) are not honest people (h)

Basic Verb "To Be" Negative Declarative: noun + location + verb "to be"			
Singular		*Plural*	
ང་གྲོང་ཁྱེར་ལ་མེད།	I am not in the city	ང་ཚོ་གྲོང་ཁྱེར་ལ་མེད།	We are not in the city
ཁྱེད་རང་ཕ་གིར་མི་འདུག ཁྱེད་རང་ཕ་གིར་ཡོད་མ་རེད།	You are not over there (h)	ཁྱེད་རང་ཚོ་ཕ་གིར་མི་འདུག ཁྱེད་རང་ཚོ་ཕ་གིར་ཡོད་མ་རེད།	You are not over there (h)
ཁོང་ཕ་གིར་མི་འདུག ཁོང་ཕ་གིར་ཡོད་མ་རེད།	She/he is not over there (h)	ཁོང་ཚོ་ཕ་གིར་མི་འདུག ཁོང་ཚོ་ཕ་གིར་ཡོད་མ་རེད།	They (m/f) are not over there (h)

Basic Verb "To Be" Negative Declarative: Possessive			
Singular		*Plural*	
ང་ལ་དངུལ་མང་པོ་མེད།	I do not have a lot of money	ང་ཚོ་ལ་དངུལ་མང་པོ་མེད།	We do not have a lot of money
ཁྱེད་རང་ལ་ཕྱུག་དངུལ་མང་པོ་མི་འདུག ཁྱེད་རང་ལ་ཕྱུག་དངུལ་མང་པོ་ཡོད་མ་རེད།	You do not have a lot of money (h)	ཁྱེད་རང་ཚོ་ལ་ཕྱུག་དངུལ་མང་པོ་མི་འདུག ཁྱེད་རང་ཚོ་ལ་ཕྱུག་དངུལ་མང་པོ་ཡོད་མ་རེད།	You do not have a lot of money (h)
ཁོང་ལ་ཕྱུག་དངུལ་མང་པོ་མི་འདུག ཁོང་ལ་ཕྱུག་དངུལ་མང་པོ་ཡོད་མ་རེད།	She/he does not have a lot of money (h)	ཁོང་ཚོ་ལ་ཕྱུག་དངུལ་མང་པོ་མི་འདུག ཁོང་ཚོ་ལ་ཕྱུག་དངུལ་མང་པོ་ཡོད་མ་རེད།	They (m/f) do not have a lot of money (h)

BASIC VERB "TO BE" AFFIRMATIVE INTERROGATIVE

Basic Verb "To Be" Affirmative Interrogative: noun + noun + verb "to be"			
Singular		*Plural*	
ང་བོད་པ་རེད་པས།	Am I a Tibetan?	ང་ཚོ་བོད་པ་རེད་པས།[1]	Are we Tibetans?
ཁྱེད་རང་བོད་པ་ཡིན་པས།	Are you a Tibetan? (h)	ཁྱེད་རང་ཚོ་བོད་པ་ཡིན་པས།	Are you Tibetans? (h)
ཁོང་བོད་པ་རེད་པས།	Is she/he a Tibetan? (h)	ཁོང་ཚོ་བོད་པ་རེད་པས།	Are they (m/f) Tibetans? (h)

---

[1] If one is asking a fellow member of the group, one could say ང་རང་ཚོ་འགྲོ་མཁན་ཡིན་པས། ("Are we goers?" or "Will we go?").

Basic Verb "To Be" Affirmative Interrogative: noun + adjective + verb "to be"			
Singular		*Plural*	
ང་དྲང་པོ་རེད་པས། ང་དྲང་པོ་འདུག་གས། ང་དྲང་པོ་ཡོད་རེད་པས།	Am I honest?	ང་ཚོ་དྲང་པོ་རེད་པས།[1] ང་ཚོ་དྲང་པོ་འདུག་གས། ང་ཚོ་དྲང་པོ་ཡོད་རེད་ པས།	Are we honest?
ཁྱེད་རང་དྲང་པོ་ཨིན་པས།	Are you honest? (h)	ཁྱེད་རང་ཚོ་དྲང་པོ་ཨིན་ པས།	Are you honest? (h)
ཁོང་དྲང་པོ་རེད་པས། ཁོང་དྲང་པོ་འདུག་གས། ཁོང་དྲང་པོ་ཡོད་རེད་པས།	Is she/he honest? (h)	ཁོང་ཚོ་དྲང་པོ་རེད་པས། ཁོང་ཚོ་དྲང་པོ་འདུག་གས། ཁོང་ཚོ་དྲང་པོ་ཡོད་རེད་ པས།	Are they (m/f) honest? (h)

---

[1] If one is asking a fellow member of the group, one also could say ང་རང་ཚོ་དྲང་པོ་ཨིན་པས། ("Are we honest?").

Basic Verb "To Be" Affirmative Interrogative: noun + noun + adjective + verb "to be"			
Singular		*Plural*	
ང་མི་དྲང་པོ་རེད་པས། ང་མི་དྲང་པོ་འདུག་གས། ང་མི་དྲང་པོ་ཡོད་རེད་ པས།	Am I an honest person?	ང་ཚོ་མི་དྲང་པོ་རེད་པས།[1] ང་ཚོ་མི་དྲང་པོ་འདུག་ གས། ང་ཚོ་མི་དྲང་པོ་ཡོད་རེད་ པས།	Are we honest people?
ཁྱེད་རང་མི་དྲང་པོ་ཨིན་ པས།	Are you an honest person? (h)	ཁྱེད་རང་ཚོ་མི་དྲང་པོ་ ཨིན་པས།	Are you honest people? (h)
ཁོང་མི་དྲང་པོ་རེད་པས། ཁོང་མི་དྲང་པོ་འདུག་གས། ཁོང་མི་དྲང་པོ་ཡོད་རེད་ པས།	Is she/he an honest person? (h)	ཁོང་ཚོ་མི་དྲང་པོ་རེད་ པས། ཁོང་ཚོ་མི་དྲང་པོ་འདུག་ གས། ཁོང་ཚོ་མི་དྲང་པོ་ཡོད་ རེད་པས།	Are they (m/f) honest people? (h)

[1] If one is asking a fellow member of the group, one also could say ང་རང་ཚོ་མི་དྲང་པོ་ཨིན་པས། ("Are we honest people?").

Basic Verb "To Be" Affirmative Interrogative: noun + location + verb "to be"			
Singular		*Plural*	
ང་གྲོང་ཁྱེར་ལ་འདུག་གསམ། ང་གྲོང་ཁྱེར་ལ་ཡོད་རེད་ པས།	Am I in the city?	ང་ཚོ་གྲོང་ཁྱེར་ལ་འདུག་ གསམ།[1] ང་ཚོ་གྲོང་ཁྱེར་ལ་ཡོད་ རེད་པས།	Are we in the city?
ཁྱེད་རང་ཕ་གིར་ཡོད་པས།	Are you over there? (h)	ཁྱེད་རང་ཚོ་ཕ་གིར་ཡོད་ པས།	Are you over there? (h)
ཁོང་ཕ་གིར་འདུག་གསམ། ཁོང་ཕ་གིར་ཡོད་རེད་པས།	Is she/he over there? (h)	ཁོང་ཚོ་ཕ་གིར་འདུག་གསམ། ཁོང་ཚོ་ཕ་གིར་ཡོད་རེད་ པས།	Are they (m/f) over there? (h)

Basic Verb "To Be" Affirmative Interrogative: Possessive			
Singular		*Plural*	
ང་ལ་དངུལ་མང་པོ་འདུག་ གསམ། ང་ལ་དངུལ་མང་པོ་ཡོད་ རེད་པས།	Do I have a lot of money?	ང་ཚོ་ལ་དངུལ་མང་པོ་ འདུག་གསམ།[2] ང་ཚོ་ལ་དངུལ་མང་པོ་ ཡོད་རེད་པས།	Do we have a lot of money?
ཁྱེད་རང་ལ་ཕྱུག་དངུལ་ མང་པོ་ཡོད་པས།	Do you have a lot of money? (h)	ཁྱེད་རང་ཚོ་ལ་ཕྱུག་དངུལ་ མང་པོ་ཡོད་པས།	Do you have a lot of money? (h)
ཁོང་ལ་ཕྱུག་དངུལ་མང་པོ་ འདུག་གསམ། ཁོང་ལ་ཕྱུག་དངུལ་མང་པོ་ ཡོད་རེད་པས།	Does she/he have a lot of money? (h)	ཁོང་ཚོ་ལ་ཕྱུག་དངུལ་མང་ པོ་འདུག་གསམ། ཁོང་ཚོ་ལ་ཕྱུག་དངུལ་མང་ པོ་ཡོད་རེད་པས།	Do they (m/f) have a lot of money? (h)

---

[1] If one is asking a fellow member of the group, one also could say ང་རང་ཚོ་འདིར་ཡོད་པས། ("Are we here?").

[2] If one is asking a fellow member of the group, one also could say ང་རང་ཚོ་ལ་དངུལ་མང་པོ་ཡོད་པས། ("Do we have a lot of money?").

BASIC VERB "TO BE" NEGATIVE INTERROGATIVE

Basic Verb "To Be" Negative Interrogative: noun + noun + verb "to be"			
Singular		*Plural*	
ང་བོད་པ་མ་རེད་པས།	Am I not a Tibetan?	ང་ཚོ་བོད་པ་མ་རེད་པས། [1]	Aren't we Tibetans?
ཁྱེད་རང་བོད་པ་མིན་པས།	Aren't you a Tibetan? (h)	ཁྱེད་རང་ཚོ་བོད་པ་མིན་ པས།	Aren't you Tibetans? (h)
ཁོང་བོད་པ་མ་རེད་པས།	Isn't she/he a Tibetan? (h)	ཁོང་ཚོ་བོད་པ་མ་རེད་ པས།	Aren't they (m/f) Tibetans? (h)

Basic Verb "To Be" Negative Interrogative: noun + adjective + verb "to be"			
Singular		*Plural*	
ང་དྲང་པོ་མ་རེད་པས། ང་དྲང་པོ་མི་འདུག་གས། ང་དྲང་པོ་ཡོད་མ་རེད་ པས།	Am I not honest?	ང་ཚོ་དྲང་པོ་མ་རེད་པས། ང་ཚོ་དྲང་པོ་མི་འདུག་ གས། ང་ཚོ་དྲང་པོ་ཡོད་མ་རེད་ པས།	Aren't we honest? [2]
ཁྱེད་རང་དྲང་པོ་མིན་པས།	Aren't you honest? (h)	ཁྱེད་རང་ཚོ་དྲང་པོ་མིན་ པས།	Aren't you honest? (h)
ཁོང་དྲང་པོ་མ་རེད་པས། ཁོང་དྲང་པོ་མི་འདུག་གས། ཁོང་དྲང་པོ་ཡོད་མ་རེད་ པས།	Isn't she/he honest? (h)	ཁོང་ཚོ་དྲང་པོ་མ་རེད་ པས། ཁོང་ཚོ་དྲང་པོ་མི་འདུག་ གས། ཁོང་ཚོ་དྲང་པོ་ཡོད་མ་ རེད་པས།	Aren't they (m/f) honest? (h)

---

[1] If one is asking a fellow member of the group, one also could say ང་རང་ཚོ་འགྲོ་མཁན་མིན་པས། ("Aren't we goers?" or "Won't we go?").

[2] If one is asking a fellow member of the group, one also could say ང་རང་ཚོ་དྲང་པོ་མིན་པས། ("Aren't we honest?").

Basic Verb "To Be" Negative Interrogative: noun + noun + adjective + verb "to be"			
Singular		*Plural*	
ང་མི་དྲང་པོ་མ་རེད་པས། ང་མི་དྲང་པོ་མི་འདུག་གས། ང་མི་དྲང་པོ་ཡོད་མ་རེད་པས།	Am I not an honest person?	ང་ཚོ་མི་དྲང་པོ་མ་རེད་པས།[1] ང་ཚོ་མི་དྲང་པོ་མི་འདུག་གས། ང་ཚོ་མི་དྲང་པོ་ཡོད་མ་རེད་པས།	Aren't we honest people?
ཁྱེད་རང་མི་དྲང་པོ་མིན་པས།	Aren't you an honest person? (h)	ཁྱེད་རང་ཚོ་མི་དྲང་པོ་མིན་པས།	Aren't you honest people? (h)
ཁོང་མི་དྲང་པོ་མ་རེད་པས། ཁོང་མི་དྲང་པོ་མི་འདུག་གས། ཁོང་མི་དྲང་པོ་ཡོད་མ་རེད་པས།	Isn't she/he an honest person? (h)	ཁོང་ཚོ་མི་དྲང་པོ་མ་རེད་པས། ཁོང་ཚོ་མི་དྲང་པོ་མི་འདུག་གས། ཁོང་ཚོ་མི་དྲང་པོ་ཡོད་མ་རེད་པས།	Aren't they (m/f) honest people? (h)

---

[1] If one is asking a fellow member of the group, one also could say ང་རང་ཚོ་མི་དྲང་པོ་མིན་པས། ("Aren't we honest people?").

Basic Verb "To Be" Negative Interrogative: noun + location + verb "to be"			
Singular		*Plural*	
ང་གྲོང་ཁྱེར་ལ་མི་འདུག་གས། ང་གྲོང་ཁྱེར་ལ་ཡོད་མ་རེད་པས།	Am I not in the city?	ང་ཚོ་གྲོང་ཁྱེར་ལ་མི་འདུག་གས།[1] ང་ཚོ་གྲོང་ཁྱེར་ལ་ཡོད་མ་རེད་པས།	Aren't we in the city?
ཁྱེད་རང་ཕ་གིར་མེད་པས།	Aren't you over there? (h)	ཁྱེད་རང་ཚོ་ཕ་གིར་མེད་པས།	Aren't you over there? (h)
ཁོང་ཕ་གིར་མི་འདུག་གས། ཁོང་ཕ་གིར་ཡོད་མ་རེད་པས།	Isn't she/he over there? (h)	ཁོང་ཚོ་ཕ་གིར་མི་འདུག་གས། ཁོང་ཚོ་ཕ་གིར་ཡོད་མ་རེད་པས།	Aren't they (m/f) over there? (h)

Basic Verb "To Be" Negative Interrogative: Possessive			
Singular		*Plural*	
ང་ལ་དངུལ་མང་པོ་མི་འདུག་གས། ང་ལ་དངུལ་མང་པོ་ཡོད་མ་རེད་པས།	Don't I have a lot of money?	ང་ཚོ་ལ་དངུལ་མང་པོ་མི་འདུག་གས།[2] ང་ཚོ་ལ་དངུལ་མང་པོ་ཡོད་མ་རེད་པས།	Don't we have a lot of money?
ཁྱེད་རང་ལ་ཕྱུག་དངུལ་མང་པོ་མེད་པས།	Don't you have a lot of money? (h)	ཁྱེད་རང་ཚོ་ལ་ཕྱུག་དངུལ་མང་པོ་མེད་པས།	Don't you have a lot of money? (h)
ཁོང་ལ་ཕྱུག་དངུལ་མང་པོ་མི་འདུག་གས། ཁོང་ལ་ཕྱུག་དངུལ་མང་པོ་ཡོད་མ་རེད་པས།	Doesn't she/he have a lot of money? (h)	ཁོང་ཚོ་ལ་ཕྱུག་དངུལ་མང་པོ་མི་འདུག་གས། ཁོང་ཚོ་ལ་ཕྱུག་དངུལ་མང་པོ་ཡོད་མ་རེད་པས།	Don't they (m/f) have a lot of money? (h)

[1] If one is asking a fellow member of the group, one also could say ང་རང་ཚོ་གྲོང་ཁྱེར་ལ་མེད་པས། ("Aren't we in the city?").

[2] If one is asking a fellow member of the group, one also could say ང་རང་ཚོ་ལ་དངུལ་མང་པོ་མེད་པས། ("Don't we have a lot of money?").

ALTERNATIVE VERB "TO BE"

There are also alternative forms of the verb "to be" for the first person declarative and second person interrogative. In these cases, third person forms of the verb "to be" are also used to de-emphasize oneself or create a sense of matter-of-factness or distance.

ALTERNATIVE VERB "TO BE" AFFIRMATIVE DECLARATIVE

Alternative Verb "To Be" Affirmative Declarative: noun + noun + verb "to be"			
Singular		Plural	
ང་བོད་པ་རེད།	I am a Tibetan	ང་ཚོ་བོད་པ་རེད།	We are Tibetans

Alternative Verb "To Be" Affirmative Declarative: noun + adjective + verb "to be"			
Singular		Plural	
ང་དྲང་པོ་རེད། ང་དྲང་པོ་ཡོད་རེད།	I am honest	ང་ཚོ་དྲང་པོ་རེད། ང་ཚོ་དྲང་པོ་ཡོད་རེད།	We are honest

Alternative Verb "To Be" Affirmative Declarative: noun + noun + adjective + verb "to be"			
Singular		Plural	
ང་མི་དྲང་པོ་རེད། ང་མི་དྲང་པོ་ཡོད་རེད།	I am an honest person	ང་ཚོ་མི་དྲང་པོ་རེད། ང་ཚོ་མི་དྲང་པོ་ཡོད་རེད།	We are honest people

Alternative Verb "To Be" Affirmative Declarative: noun + location + verb "to be"			
Singular		Plural	
ང་གྲོང་ཁྱེར་ལ་ཡོད་རེད།	I am in the city	ང་ཚོ་གྲོང་ཁྱེར་ལ་ཡོད་ རེད།	We are in the city

Alternative Verb "To Be" Affirmative Declarative: Possessive			
Singular		Plural	
ང་ལ་དངུལ་མང་པོ་ཡོད་ རེད།	I have a lot of money	ང་ཚོ་ལ་དངུལ་མང་པོ་ ཡོད་རེད།	We have a lot of money

ALTERNATIVE VERB "TO BE" NEGATIVE DECLARATIVE

Alternative Verb "To Be" Negative Declarative: noun + noun + verb "to be"			
Singular		*Plural*	
ང་བོད་པ་མ་རེད།	I am not a Tibetan	ང་ཚོ་བོད་པ་མ་རེད།	We aren't Tibetans

Alternative Verb "To Be" Negative Declarative: noun + adjective + verb "to be"			
Singular		*Plural*	
ང་དྲང་པོ་མ་རེད། ང་དྲང་པོ་ཡོད་མ་རེད།	I am not honest	ང་ཚོ་དྲང་པོ་མ་རེད། ང་ཚོ་དྲང་པོ་ཡོད་མ་རེད།	We are not honest

Alternative Verb "To Be" Negative Declarative: noun + noun + adjective + verb "to be"			
Singular		*Plural*	
ང་མི་དྲང་པོ་མ་རེད། ང་མི་དྲང་པོ་ཡོད་མ་རེད།	I am not an honest person	ང་ཚོ་མི་དྲང་པོ་མ་རེད། ང་ཚོ་མི་དྲང་པོ་ཡོད་མ་རེད།	We are not honest people

Alternative Verb "To Be" Negative Declarative: noun + location + verb "to be"			
Singular		*Plural*	
ང་གྲོང་ཁྱེར་ལ་ཡོད་མ་རེད།	I am not in the city	ང་ཚོ་གྲོང་ཁྱེར་ལ་ཡོད་མ་རེད།	We are not in the city

Alternative Verb "To Be" Negative Declarative: Possessive			
Singular		*Plural*	
ང་ལ་དངུལ་མང་པོ་ཡོད་མ་རེད།	I don't have a lot of money	ང་ཚོ་ལ་དངུལ་མང་པོ་ཡོད་མ་རེད།	We don't have a lot of money

ALTERNATIVE VERB "TO BE" AFFIRMATIVE INTERROGATIVE

Alternative Verb "To Be" Affirmative Interrogative: noun + noun + verb "to be"			
Singular		*Plural*	
ཁྱེད་རང་བོད་པ་རེད་པས།	Are you a Tibetan? (h)	ཁྱེད་རང་ཚོ་བོད་པ་རེད་པས།	Are you Tibetans? (h)

Alternative Verb "To Be" Affirmative Interrogative: noun + adjective + verb "to be"			
Singular		*Plural*	
ཁྱེད་རང་དྲང་པོ་རེད་པས། ཁྱེད་རང་དྲང་པོ་ཡིན་རེད་པས།	Are you honest? (h)	ཁྱེད་རང་ཚོ་དྲང་པོ་རེད་པས། ཁྱེད་རང་ཚོ་དྲང་པོ་ཡིན་རེད་པས།	Are you honest? (h)

Alternative Verb "To Be" Affirmative Interrogative: noun + noun + adjective + verb "to be"			
Singular		*Plural*	
ཁྱེད་རང་མི་དྲང་པོ་རེད་པས། ཁྱེད་རང་མི་དྲང་པོ་ཡིན་རེད་པས།	Are you an honest person? (h)	ཁྱེད་རང་ཚོ་མི་དྲང་པོ་རེད་པས། ཁྱེད་རང་ཚོ་མི་དྲང་པོ་ཡིན་རེད་པས།	Are you honest people? (h)

Alternative Verb "To Be" Affirmative Interrogative: noun + location + verb "to be"			
Singular		*Plural*	
ཁྱེད་རང་གྲོང་ཁྱེར་ལ་ཡོད་རེད་པས།	Are you in the city? (h)	ཁྱེད་རང་ཚོ་གྲོང་ཁྱེར་ལ་ཡོད་རེད་པས།	Are you in the city? (h)

Alternative Verb "To Be" Affirmative Interrogative: Possessive			
Singular		*Plural*	
ཁྱེད་རང་ལ་ཕྱུག་དངུལ་མང་པོ་ཡོད་རེད་པས།	Do you have a lot of money? (h)	ཁྱེད་རང་ཚོ་ལ་ཕྱུག་དངུལ་མང་པོ་ཡོད་རེད་པས།	Do you have a lot of money? (h)

ALTERNATIVE VERB "TO BE" NEGATIVE INTERROGATIVE

Alternative Verb "To Be" Negative Interrogative: noun + noun + verb "to be"			
Singular		*Plural*	
ཁྱེད་རང་བོད་པ་མ་རེད་པས།	Aren't you a Tibetan?	ཁྱེད་རང་ཚོ་བོད་པ་མ་རེད་པས།	Aren't you Tibetan?

Alternative Verb "To Be" Negative Interrogative: noun + adjective + verb "to be"			
Singular		*Plural*	
ཁྱེད་རང་དྲང་པོ་མ་རེད་ པས། ཁྱེད་རང་དྲང་པོ་ཡོད་མ་ རེད་པས།	Aren't you honest? (h)	ཁྱེད་རང་ཚོ་དྲང་པོ་མ་རེད་ པས། ཁྱེད་རང་ཚོ་དྲང་པོ་ཡོད་ མ་རེད་པས།	Aren't you honest? (h)

Alternative Verb "To Be" Negative Interrogative: noun + noun + adjective + verb "to be"			
Singular		*Plural*	
ཁྱེད་རང་མི་དྲང་པོ་མ་རེད་ པས། ཁྱེད་རང་མི་དྲང་པོ་ཡོད་ མ་རེད་པས།	Aren't you an honest person? (h)	ཁྱེད་རང་ཚོ་མི་དྲང་པོ་མ་ རེད་པས། ཁྱེད་རང་ཚོ་མི་དྲང་པོ་ ཡོད་མ་རེད་པས།	Aren't you honest people? (h)

Alternative Verb "To Be" Negative Interrogative: noun + location + verb "to be"			
Singular		*Plural*	
ཁྱེད་རང་གྲོང་ཁྱེར་ལ་ཡོད་ མ་རེད་པས།	Aren't you in the city? (h)	ཁྱེད་རང་ཚོ་གྲོང་ཁྱེར་ལ་ ཡོད་མ་རེད་པས།	Aren't you in the city? (h)

Alternative Verb "To Be" Negative Interrogative: Possessive			
Singular		*Plural*	
ཁྱེད་རང་ལ་ཕྱུག་དངུལ་ མང་པོ་ཡོད་མ་རེད་པས།	Don't you have a lot of money? (h)	ཁྱེད་རང་ཚོ་ལ་ཕྱུག་དངུལ་ མང་པོ་ཡོད་མ་རེད་པས།	Don't you have a lot of money? (h)

REPEATING THE VERB "TO BE" TO INDICATE ENTHUSIASM

In the Unit 11 dialogue when Dé-g̱yí asks ཁྱེད་རང་བོད་ཇ་མཆོད་ཀས། ("Will you drink Tibetan tea?" h), Sö'-nam replies ཡིན་ཡིན། བོད་ཇ་འཐུང་གི་ཡིན། ("Yes, Yes. I will drink Tibetan tea"). The repetition of ཡིན་ conveys a sense of enthusiasm or eagerness. Similarly, if one were to be asked དོ་དགོང་གློག་བརྙན་ལ་ཕེབས་ཀས། ("Will you go to the movies tonight?" h), one might respond ཡིན་ཡིན། ང་འགྲོ་གི་ཡིན། ("Yes, yes. I will go"). The expressions ཡིན་དག་ཡིན་ ("certainly") and ཡིན་དག་མིན་ ("obviously") are also used to indicate enthusiasm. It might seem counter-intuitive that ཡིན་དག་ཡིན་ and ཡིན་དག་མིན་ would both have relatively the same meaning since the latter contains a negative; however, the latter most likely means "There is no need to talk about whether or not [such and such]" in the sense that it is certainly so. For drills see Unit 11.5.

FUTURE TENSE

Unit 6 introduces the future tense. It correlates to the simple future in English and, in some cases of verbs of going, to the present continuous. For instance, in the dialogue Bé'-ma says to Gël-sang ཁྱེད་རང་ག་པར་ཕེབས་ཀ| ("Where are you going?" h), meaning "Where are you going *right now*?". The form used in Tibetan is the future tense, most likely because the destination will be reached in the future, but in English the present continuous is used. Since in Tibetan the main usage of the form is future—"He/she will...", in this text it usually is translated that way. However, keep in mind that for verbs of going it can mean the present continuous.

We will use the English convention of conjugating verbs in the first, second, and third persons, but it should be understood that because of the downplaying of the self in Tibetan culture there is no layout corresponding to a system in which oneself is the first person. If anything, others are the first person, and oneself is in a secondary category.

FUTURE TENSE: BASIC FORMS
The future tense is built using the future form of the verb plus the particle གི (or its equivalents གྱི and ཀྱི)[1] and an auxiliary verb. For first person, the auxiliary verb is ཡིན and for second and third persons, the auxiliary verb is རེད.

Basic Future: Affirmative Declarative			
Singular		*Plural*	
ང་འགྲོ་གི་ཡིན|	I will go	ང་ཚོ་འགྲོ་གི་ཡིན|	We will go
ཁྱེད་རང་ཕེབས་ཀྱི་རེད|	You will go (h)	ཁྱེད་རང་ཚོ་ཕེབས་ཀྱི་རེད|	You will go (h)
ཁོང་ཕེབས་ཀྱི་རེད|	She/he will go (h)	ཁོང་ཚོ་ཕེབས་ཀྱི་རེད|	They (m/f) will go (h)

Although the full paradigm of the future tense is given in the chart, in actual usage the second person declarative form is seldom used. Rather, conversation involving the second

---

[1] As with the genitive endings, གི follows the suffixes ག and ང; གྱི follows ན མ ར and ལ; and ཀྱི follows ད བ and ས. In literary Tibetan the suffix འ becomes འི, and words without a suffix are followed by འི or ཡི, but in the spoken language this distinction is not closely followed, and གི is often used.

person tends to revolve around questions, such as ག་པར་ཕེབས་ཀ། ("Where will you go?" or "Where are you going?" h) or ཁྲོམ་ལ་ཕེབས་ཀྱི་ཡིན་པས། ("Will you go to the market?" or "Are you going to the market?" h). Since the aim of this book is to teach the language as it is actually used, second person forms are drilled here mainly in the interrogative. Also, for the second and third persons, this text concentrates primarily on the honorific pronouns since they are used more frequently and since it is important to become accustomed to two ways of expressing the same meaning, honorifically and non-honorifically.

Interrogative: The second person uses the third person auxiliary verb ending རེད་ for declarative statements, as in ཁྱེད་རང་ཕེབས་ཀྱི་རེད། ("You will go" h), and uses the first person auxiliary verb ending ཡིན་ for the interrogative, as in ཁྱེད་རང་ཕེབས་ཀྱི་ཡིན་པས། ("Will you go?" or "Are you going?" h). (Note that the contracted form of ཁྱེད་རང་ཕེབས་ཀྱི་ཡིན་པས། is ཁྱེད་རང་ཕེབས་ཀས།.) Therefore, we refer to the two forms གི་ཡིན་ and གི་རེད་ respectively as the first person form and the third person form. To repeat: Second person declarative statements use the third person auxiliary verb ending རེད་, and second person interrogatives use the first person auxiliary verb ending ཡིན་. The latter is in deference to the other person, since that person will use the first person auxiliary verb in her or his reply; for instance, one says ཁྱེད་ རང་ཁྲོམ་ལ་ཕེབས་ཀྱི་ཡིན་པས། ("Will you go to the market?" or "Are you going to the market?") so that it accords with the form in which the answer will be given— ང་ཁྲོམ་ལ་འགྲོ་གི་ཡིན། ("I will go to the market" or "I am going to the market"). The same principle is used for first person questions; the auxiliary verb ending རེད་ is used because the answer will be given in the second person, as in ང་འགྲོ་གི་རེད་པས། ("Will I go?") which is answered ཁྱེད་རང་ཕེབས་ཀྱི་ རེད། ("You will go").

Basic Future: Affirmative Interrogative			
Singular		*Plural*	
ང་འགྲོ་གི་རེད་པས།	Will I go?	ང་ཚོ་འགྲོ་གི་རེད་པས།[1]	Will we go?
ཁྱེད་རང་ཕེབས་ཀྱི་ཡིན་ པས།	Will you go? (h)	ཁྱེད་རང་ཚོ་ཕེབས་ཀྱི་ཡིན་ པས།	Will you go? (h)
ཁྱེད་རང་ཕེབས་ཀས།		ཁྱེད་རང་ཚོ་ཕེབས་ཀས།	
ཁོང་ཕེབས་ཀྱི་རེད་པས།	Will she/he go? (h)	ཁོང་ཚོ་ཕེབས་ཀྱི་རེད་པས།	Will they (m/f) go? (h)

---

[1] If one is asking a fellow member of the group, one also could say ང་རང་ཚོ་འགྲོ་གི་ཡིན་པས། or ང་རང་ཚོ་འགྲོ་གས།.

For drills see Unit 6.7-6.22, 7.49-7.51, 10.31-10.39, 10.45-10.46, 12.109-12.110.

The question in the first line of the dialogue in Unit 7 ཁྱེད་རང་ག་རེ་གཉགས་ཀྱི་ཡིན་པ། "What will you buy?" h) is the full version of the second person interrogative form. In Unit 6 the contracted form appeared in the question ག་པར་ཕེབས་ཀ། ("Where are you going?" h), and the contracted form is also used in Unit 7 in the question ག་རེ་གཉགས་ཀ། ("What will you buy?" h). The expanded versions of these are ག་རེ་གཉགས་ཀྱི་ཡིན་པ། and ག་པར་ཕེབས་ཀྱི་ཡིན་པ།. In the expanded form it is easy to see the structure of the pattern: an interrogative pronoun, a future tense verb, and the particle པ་ which is used with questions having an interrogative pronoun. For drills see Unit 7.49-7.51, 10.31-10.32, 10.36.

NEGATIVE OF THE FUTURE TENSE: BASIC FORM

The negative of the future tense is built like the affirmative except that, in the first person the negative auxiliary verb མེན་ is used instead of ཡིན་ and in the second and third person the negative auxiliary verb is མ་རེད་.

Basic Future: Negative Declarative			
Singular		*Plural*	
ང་འགྲོ་གི་མེན།	I will not go	ང་ཚོ་འགྲོ་གི་མེན།	We will not go
ཁྱེད་རང་ཕེབས་ཀྱི་མ་རེད།	You will not go (h)	ཁྱེད་རང་ཚོ་ཕེབས་ཀྱི་མ་རེད།	You will not go (h)
ཁོང་ཕེབས་ཀྱི་མ་རེད།	She/he will not go (h)	ཁོང་ཚོ་ཕེབས་ཀྱི་མ་རེད།	They (m/f) will not go (h)

Interrogative: The interrogative adds the question particle པས་. Just as second person interrogatives use first person endings because they will be answered in the first person, so, first person interrogatives use second person endings because they will be answered in the second person.

Basic Future: Negative Interrogative			
Singular		*Plural*	
ང་འགྲོ་གི་མ་རེད་པས།	Won't I go?	ང་ཚོ་འགྲོ་གི་མ་རེད་པས།[1]	Won't we go?
ཁྱེད་རང་ཕེབས་ཀྱི་མེན་པས།[2]	Won't you go? (h)	ཁྱེད་རང་ཚོ་ཕེབས་ཀྱི་མེན་པས།[3]	Won't you go? (h)
ཁོང་ཕེབས་ཀྱི་མ་རེད་པས།	Won't she/he go? (h)	ཁོང་ཚོ་ཕེབས་ཀྱི་མ་རེད་པས།	Won't they (m/f) go? (h)

For drills see Unit 6.23-6.35.

In English and in Tibetan, negative questions can call for either affirmative or negative replies, according to context. In Tibetan, མ་རེད་པས་ and མེན་པས་ are used to form negative questions. To reply in the affirmative, one constructs a simple declarative sentence, omitting the negative particle. For instance, if asked ཁང་པ་འདི་གསར་པ་མ་རེད་པས། ("Isn't this house new?"), one could reply in the affirmative ལགས་གསར་པ་རེད། ཁང་པ་འདི་གསར་པ་རེད། ("Yes, [it] is new; this house is new"). Negative questions in the second person end with མེན་པས་ rather than མ་རེད་པས་. For instance, the question might be ཁྱེད་རང་དངུལ་ཁང་ལ་ཕེབས་ཀྱི་མེན་པས། ("Won't you go to the bank?" h), to which one could reply ལགས་འགྲོ་གི་ཡིན། དངུལ་ཁང་ལ་འགྲོ་གི་ཡིན། ("Yes, I will go; I will go to the bank"). Sometimes the negative question form is used for emphasis, and sometimes it is an actual question; if it is the latter, the intonation should rise at the end of the sentence. For drills, see Unit 9.49-9.51.

FUTURE TENSE: ALTERNATIVE FORMS

There are also alternative future verb forms. These are of three types:

1 changing auxiliary verbs in the first person singular and plural to de-emphasize

---

[1] If one is asking a fellow member of the group, one also could say ང་རང་ཚོ་འགྲོ་གི་མེན་པས. It might seem that the shortened form of the latter, ང་རང་ཚོ་མ་འགྲོ་གས, would have the same meaning, but it does not; rather, it means "Might we not go?" with the sense that the speaker wishes that they not go.

[2] It might seem that the shortened form of this, ཁྱེད་རང་མ་ཕེབས་གས, would have the same meaning, but it does not; rather, it means "Might you not go?" with the sense that the speaker wishes that the person not go.

[3] It might seem that the shortened form of this, ཁྱེད་རང་ཚོ་མ་ཕེབས་གས, would have the same meaning, but it does not; it means "Might you not go?" with the sense that the speaker wishes that the persons not go.

intentionality.

2   changing from non-honorific to honorific verbs in the first person plural to honor the other members of your esteemed group.

3   changing from honorific to non-honorific pronouns and verbs in the second and third person singular and plural to speak in a common manner.

ALTERNATIVE FUTURE: DE-EMPHASIZING FIRST PERSON INTENTIONALITY

The third person auxiliary verb ending གི་རེད་ is used quite often for the first person to de-emphasize the intentionality of the agent of the verb, "I" or "we". For instance ང་ཁྲོམ་ལ་འགྲོ་གི་ཡིན། ("I will go to the market" or "I am going to the market") is more assertive and indicates that it is one's own decision, whereas ང་ཁྲོམ་ལ་འགྲོ་གི་རེད། ("I will go to the market")[1] is less assertive and can indicate that one's going depends upon conditions or will occur along the way. Note that the form with གི་རེད་ is used only for the future and not for actions that are currently taking place.

Alternative Future: De-Emphasizing First Person Intentionality: Affirmative Declarative			
Singular		*Plural*	
ང་འགྲོ་གི་རེད།	I will go	ང་ཚོ་འགྲོ་གི་རེད།	We will go

The negative of the alternative forms of the future tense is built like the affirmative except that the negative auxiliary verb མ་རེད་ is used.

Alternative Future: De-Emphasizing First Person Intentionality: Negative Declarative			
Singular		*Plural*	
ང་འགྲོ་གི་མ་རེད།	I will not go	ང་ཚོ་འགྲོ་གི་མ་རེད།	We will not go

For drills see Unit 6.36-6.38.

ALTERNATIVE FUTURE: HONORING THE OTHER MEMBERS OF YOUR ESTEEMED GROUP

Tibetans do not use honorific forms for the first person singular but to respect others will sometimes employ the honorific in the first person plural. Hence, when one is in groups

---

[1] It is for a similar reason that in first person statements Tibetans often drop the agent altogether, no matter what auxiliary verb form they are using. Thus, if the auxiliary verb form communicates who the agent is, as in ཁྲོམ་ལ་འགྲོ་གི་ཡིན། ("I will go to the market"), the subject is most frequently dropped.

that include esteemed persons, such as one's parents, teachers, ordained persons, government officials, and so forth, one can use an honorific verb form for the first person plural, since the reference of the honorific is not to oneself but to others in the group.[1] Therefore, instead of འགྲོ་, the common form of the verb "to go", one uses ཕེབས་, the honorific form. Also, in order to be less assertive, one uses the third person auxiliary verb ending ཀྱི་རེད་, making ང་ཚོ་ཕེབས་ཀྱི་རེད། ("We will go").

Alternative Future: Honoring Your Group: Affirmative Declarative		
Singular	*Plural*	
	ང་ཚོ་ཕེབས་ཀྱི་རེད།	We will go (h)

Interrogative: The interrogative adds the question particle པས་. Just as second person interrogatives use first person endings because they will be answered in the first person, so, first person interrogatives use second person endings because they will be answered in the second person.

Alternative Future: Honoring Your Group: Affirmative Interrogative		
Singular	*Plural*	
	ང་ཚོ་ཕེབས་ཀྱི་རེད་པས།[2]	Will we go? (h)

Alternative Future: Honoring Your Group: Negative Declarative		
Singular	*Plural*	
	ང་ཚོ་ཕེབས་ཀྱི་མ་རེད།	We will not go (h)

Alternative Future: Honoring Your Group: Negative Interrogative		
Singular	*Plural*	
	ང་ཚོ་ཕེབས་ཀྱི་མ་རེད་ པས།[3]	Won't we go? (h)

---

[1] Nevertheless, some Tibetans find it uncomfortable to refer to themselves with the honorific and so find other ways to express honorific first-person plural constructions.

[2] If one is asking a fellow member of the group, one also could say ང་རང་ཚོ་ཕེབས་ཀྱི་ཡིན་པས། or ང་རང་ཚོ་ཕེབས་གས།

[3] If one is asking a fellow member of the group, one also could say ང་རང་ཚོ་ཕེབས་ཀྱི་མིན་པས།. It might seem that the shortened form of the latter, ང་རང་ཚོ་མ་ཕེབས་གས།, would have the same meaning, but it does not; rather, it

For drills see Unit 6.39-6.44.

ALTERNATIVE FUTURE: NON-HONORIFIC SECOND AND THIRD PERSON

Since honorifics show respect for equals, superiors, or anyone to whom you wish to show deference, they should be used in almost all situations. Therefore, as was indicated earlier, a good rule of thumb is to use them whenever either directly addressing or speaking of someone else. Still, it is important to know how to use non-honorific forms of the second and third person (in addition to those for the first person which you normally should use) since some people, especially those from the southeastern province of Kam (ཁམས་) , use few or no honorifics. For the third person one simply uses the non-honorific personal pronouns མོ་ and ཁོ་ with the non-honorific form of the verb, in this instance འགྲོ, and the third person ending གི་རེད་ making མོ་འགྲོ་གི་རེད། ("She will go") and ཁོ་འགྲོ་གི་རེད། ("He will go"). Second person declarative statements are formed in the same way as they are for the third person, making ཁྱེད་འགྲོ་གི་རེད། ("You will go").

Alternative Future: Non-Honorific Second and Third Person: Affirmative Declarative			
Singular		*Plural*	
ཁྱེད་རང་འགྲོ་གི་རེད།	You will go	ཁྱེད་རང་ཚོ་འགྲོ་གི་རེད།	You will go
ཁོ་འགྲོ་གི་རེད།	He will go	ཁོ་ཚོ་འགྲོ་གི་རེད།	They will go
མོ་འགྲོ་གི་རེད།	She will go	མོ་རང་ཚོ་འགྲོ་གི་རེད།[1]	They will go

---

means "Might we not go?" with the sense that the speaker wishes that they not go.

[1] The feminine plural pronoun མོ་རང་ཚོ་ is very rare; some Central Tibetans advocate not using it at all; in place of it they use ཁོ་ཚོ་ .

Interrogative: The interrogative adds the question particle པས་.

<table>
<tr><td colspan="4" align="center">Alternative Future: Non-Honorific Second and Third Person: Affirmative Interrogative</td></tr>
<tr><td colspan="2" align="center">Singular</td><td colspan="2" align="center">Plural</td></tr>
<tr><td>ཁྱོད་རང་འགྲོ་གི་ཡིན་པས།
 ཁྱོད་རང་འགྲོ་གས།</td><td>Will you go?</td><td>ཁྱོད་རང་ཚོ་འགྲོ་གི་ཡིན་ པས།
 ཁྱོད་རང་ཚོ་འགྲོ་གས།</td><td>Will you go?</td></tr>
<tr><td>ཁོ་འགྲོ་གི་རེད་པས།</td><td>Will he go?</td><td>ཁོ་ཚོ་འགྲོ་གི་རེད་པས།</td><td>Will they go?</td></tr>
<tr><td>མོ་འགྲོ་གི་རེད་པས།</td><td>Will she go?</td><td>མོ་རང་ཚོ་འགྲོ་གི་རེད་ པས།[1]</td><td>Will they go?</td></tr>
</table>

Negative: The negative of the alternative forms of the future tense is built like the affirmative except that the negative auxiliary verb མ་རེད་ is used for all persons.

<table>
<tr><td colspan="4" align="center">Alternative Future: Non-Honorific Second and Third Person: Negative Declarative</td></tr>
<tr><td colspan="2" align="center">Singular</td><td colspan="2" align="center">Plural</td></tr>
<tr><td>ཁྱོད་རང་འགྲོ་གི་མ་རེད།</td><td>You will not go</td><td>ཁྱོད་རང་ཚོ་འགྲོ་གི་མ་ རེད།</td><td>You will not go</td></tr>
<tr><td>ཁོ་འགྲོ་གི་མ་རེད།</td><td>He will not go</td><td>ཁོ་ཚོ་འགྲོ་གི་མ་རེད།</td><td>They will not go</td></tr>
<tr><td>མོ་འགྲོ་གི་མ་རེད།</td><td>She will not go</td><td>མོ་རང་ཚོ་འགྲོ་གི་མ་རེད།[2]</td><td>They will not go</td></tr>
</table>

---

[1] The feminine plural pronoun མོ་རང་ཚོ་ is very rare; some Central Tibetans advocate not using it at all; in place of it they use ཁོ་ཚོ་.

[2] The feminine plural pronoun མོ་རང་ཚོ་ is very rare; some Central Tibetans advocate not using it at all; in place of it they use ཁོ་ཚོ་.

Interrogative: The interrogative adds the question particle པས་.

<table>
<tr><td colspan="4" align="center">Alternative Future: Non-Honorific Second and Third Person: Negative Interrogative</td></tr>
<tr><td colspan="2" align="center">Singular</td><td colspan="2" align="center">Plural</td></tr>
<tr><td>ཁྱེད་རང་འགྲོ་གི་མེན་ པས།[1]</td><td>Won't you go?</td><td>ཁྱེད་རང་ཚོ་འགྲོ་གི་མེན་ པས།[2]</td><td>Won't you go?</td></tr>
<tr><td>ཁོ་འགྲོ་གི་མ་རེད་པས།</td><td>Won't he go?</td><td>ཁོ་ཚོ་འགྲོ་གི་མ་རེད་པས།</td><td>Won't they go?</td></tr>
<tr><td>མོ་འགྲོ་གི་མ་རེད་པས།</td><td>Won't she go?</td><td>མོ་རང་ཚོ་འགྲོ་གི་མ་རེད་ པས།[3]</td><td>Won't they go?</td></tr>
</table>

For drills see Unit 6.45-6.55.

For summary drills for the future tense see Unit 6.56-6.58. For more future drills see Unit 7.5-7.29 and 7.49-7.52.

FUTURE VERB FORMS WITH མཁན་ AND ཆེན་

The basic future construction is verb plus auxiliary གི་ཡིན་ or གི་རེད་, as in ང་འགྲོ་གི་ཡིན། ("I will go") and ཁོང་ཕེབས་ཀྱི་རེད། ("He will go" h). An alternate construction uses verb plus མཁན་ཡིན་, མཁན་རེད་, ཆེན་ཡིན་, or ཆེན་རེད་,[4] as in ང་འགྲོ་མཁན་ཡིན། ("I will go"), ང་འགྲོ་ཆེན་ཡིན། ("I will go"), ཁོང་ཕེབས་མཁན་རེད། ("She will go" h), and ཁོང་ཕེབས་ཆེན་རེད། ("He will go" h). As you will remember, མཁན་ is used to form verbal agent nouns; thus, a super-literal translation of ང་འགྲོ་མཁན་ཡིན། might be "I am the goer," and of ཁོང་ཕེབས་ཆེན་རེད།, "She is the goer" (h); however, to say "I am the one who is going" one adds དེ་, as in ང་འགྲོ་མཁན་དེ་ ཡིན།, and to say "She is the one who is going" one says ཁོང་ཕེབས་ཆེན་དེ་རེད།. Therefore, this construction without དེ་ is better understood as another way of forming the future tense.[5]

---

[1] It might seem that the shortened form of this, ཁྱེད་རང་མ་འགྲོ་གས།, would have the same meaning, but it does not; rather, it means "Might you not go?" with the sense that the speaker wishes that the person not go.

[2] It might seem that the shortened form of this, ཁྱེད་རང་ཚོ་མ་འགྲོ་གས།, would have the same meaning, but it does not; rather, it means "Might you not go?" with the sense that the speaker wishes that the person not go.

[3] The feminine plural pronoun མོ་རང་ཚོ་ is very rare; some Central Tibetans advocate not using it at all; in place of it they use ཁོ་ཚོ་.

[4] Sometimes these are pronounced as ངན་ཡིན་ and ངན་རེད་ .

[5] Nevertheless, that it is not always the same as the future is indicated by its being used for "I am the one to go to the market, but I will not go" —ང་ཁྲོམ་ལ་འགྲོ་མཁན་ཡིན་ཀྱང་ང་འགྲོ་གི་མེན།.

For drills see Unit 7.37-7.48.

PRESENT TENSE

The Unit 12 dialogue begins with <u>D</u>or-jé asking ཐོམ་ལགས། ཁྱེད་རང་དེང་སང་ག་རེ་གནང་གི་ཡོད།
("Tom, what are you doing nowadays?" h). Tom replies ང་དེང་སང་བོད་སྐད་བསླབ་ཀྱི་ཡོད།
("Nowadays I am studying Tibetan"). Their exchange introduces the form and use of the
present tense. To learn the present tense, we need to consider the way in which verbs of
action are constructed.

PRESENT TENSE: BASIC FORMS

In conversation the future, present, and past tenses of Tibetan verbs are indicated through
the use of different auxiliary verb endings and through changes in the form of the main
verb. You have learned to use the future tense with verbs of action. In Unit 6 you learned ང་
ཁྲོམ་ལ་འགྲོ་གི་ཡིན། ("I will go to the market"); in Unit 7, ཁོང་གིས་ཤིང་ཏོག་གཉིས་ཀྱི་རེད། ("He will
buy fruit" h); in Unit 9, ཁོང་གཉིས་ཁང་ལ་ཕེབས་ཀྱི་རེད། ("She will go home" h); in Unit 10, ང་
འབྲས་བཟའ་གི་ཡིན། ("I will eat rice"); and in Unit 11, ང་བོད་ཇ་འཐུང་གི་ཡིན། ("I will drink Tibetan
tea"). In these sentences, the auxiliary verb ཡིན་ or རེད་ is attached to the main verbs འགྲོ་,
གཉིས་, ཕེབས་, བཟའ་, and འཐུང་ by a connective particle—གི་, ཀྱི་, or གྱི་—to form the future
tense. The form of the main verb frequently does not vary from tense to tense, and many of
the changes that the main verb does undergo cannot be heard or can be heard only with
difficulty. For these reasons, it is principally the auxiliary verb that signals the tense to the
listener. The future tense, as we have heard and seen, uses the auxiliary verbs ཡིན་ and རེད་.
The present tense uses the auxiliary verbs ཡོད་, འདུག་, and ཡོད་རེད་.

First person. The auxiliary verb ཡོད་ is used with first person expressions or when asking a question that will be answered in the first person. For instance, to say, "Nowadays I
am studying Tibetan," one uses the auxiliary verb ཡོད་, because the expression is stated in
the first person, and combines it with the main verb བསླབ་,[1] making ང་དེང་སང་བོད་སྐད་བསླབ་ཀྱི་
ཡོད། ("Nowadays I am studying Tibetan"). Similarly, because the question "What are you
doing nowadays?" will be answered in the first person, one uses the auxiliary ཡོད་ as in ཁྱེད་
རང་དེང་སང་ག་རེ་གནང་གི་ཡོད། ("What are you doing nowadays?" h). In the negative, མེད་
replaces ཡོད་; therefore, Tom says ངས་ཡག་པོ་ཤེས་ཀྱི་མེད། ("I do not know [it] well"). For
drills see Unit 12.5-12.7, 12.19-12.20, 12.50-12.51, 12.60-12.61.

---

[1] Although the actual present tense form of the verb "to study" is སྦྱ་, most Tibetans say བསླབ་ (the future
tense form) for the present, and therefore we will use this form.

Second person. Second person expressions use the auxiliary verbs འདུག and ཡོད་རེད་ (except, as we have just seen, for those occasions when one is posing a question that will be answered in the first person). For instance, to praise Tom's spoken Tibetan, D̲or-jé says ཁྱེད་རང་བོད་སྐད་ཡག་པོ་མཁྱེན་གྱི་འདུག ("You know Tibetan well" h) and could have said ཁྱེད་རང་བོད་སྐད་ཡག་པོ་མཁྱེན་གྱི་ཡོད་རེད། For drills see Unit 12.8-12.11, 12.19-12.20, 12.52-12.53, 12.62-12.63.

Third person. When speaking about a third person, one says ཁོང་བོད་སྐད་ཡག་པོ་མཁྱེན་གྱི་འདུག or ཁོང་བོད་སྐད་ཡག་པོ་མཁྱེན་གྱི་ཡོད་རེད། ("He knows Tibetan well" h). For both the second and third person one joins the auxiliary verbs འདུག or ཡོད་རེད་ to a main verb such as མཁྱེན་ with the connective particle གྱི, ཀྱི, or གི to form the present tense verb, as in མཁྱེན་གྱི་འདུག or མཁྱེན་གྱི་ཡོད་རེད། If one wishes to ask a question about a third person, one adds the question particle གས or པས as in ཁོང་བོད་སྐད་ཡག་པོ་མཁྱེན་གྱི་འདུག་གས or ཁོང་བོད་སྐད་ཡག་པོ་མཁྱེན་གྱི་ཡོད་རེད་པས ("Does she know Tibetan well?" h). For drills see Unit 12.12-12.18, 12.19-12.20, 12.54-12.55, 12.65-12.66.

Basic Present: Affirmative Declarative			
Singular		*Plural*	
ངས་ལས་ཀ་བྱེད་ཀྱི་ཡོད།	I work/ I am working/ I do work	ང་ཚོས་ལས་ཀ་བྱེད་ཀྱི་ཡོད།	We work/ We are working/ We do work
ཁྱེད་རང་གིས་ཕྱག་ལས་གནང་གི་འདུག ཁྱེད་རང་གིས་ཕྱག་ལས་གནང་གི་ཡོད་རེད།	You work/ You are working/ You do work (h)	ཁྱེད་རང་ཚོས་ཕྱག་ལས་གནང་གི་འདུག ཁྱེད་རང་ཚོས་ཕྱག་ལས་གནང་གི་ཡོད་རེད།	You work/ You are working/ You do work (h)
ཁོང་གིས་ཕྱག་ལས་གནང་གི་འདུག ཁོང་གིས་ཕྱག་ལས་གནང་གི་ཡོད་རེད།	She/he works/ He/she is working/ She/he does work (h)	ཁོང་ཚོས་ཕྱག་ལས་གནང་གི་འདུག ཁོང་ཚོས་ཕྱག་ལས་གནང་གི་ཡོད་རེད།	They (m/f) work/ They are working/ They do work (h)

Basic Present: Affirmative Interrogative			
Singular		*Plural*	
ངས་ལས་ཀ་བྱེད་ཀྱི་འདུག་གས། ངས་ལས་ཀ་བྱེད་ཀྱི་ཡོད་རེད་པས།	Do I work?/ Am I work-ing?	ང་ཚོས་ལས་ཀ་བྱེད་ཀྱི་འདུག་གས།[1] ང་ཚོས་ལས་ཀ་བྱེད་ཀྱི་ཡོད་རེད་པས།	Do we work?/ Are we working?
ཁྱེད་རང་གིས་ཕྱག་ལས་གནང་གི་ཡོད་པས།	Do you work?/ Are you working? (h)	ཁྱེད་རང་ཚོས་ཕྱག་ལས་གནང་གི་ཡོད་པས།	Do you work?/ Are you working? (h)
ཁོང་གིས་ཕྱག་ལས་གནང་གི་འདུག་གས། ཁོང་གིས་ཕྱག་ལས་གནང་གི་ཡོད་རེད་པས།	Does she/he work?/ Is he/she working? (h)	ཁོང་ཚོས་ཕྱག་ལས་གནང་གི་འདུག་གས། ཁོང་ཚོས་ཕྱག་ལས་གནང་གི་ཡོད་རེད་པས།	Do they (m/f) work?/ Are they working? (h)

SUMMATION OF BASIC PRESENT VERB FORMS

The use of auxiliaries in present tense declarative statements is simple: with the appropriate connective particle (གི , གྱི, or གྱི) use ཡོད་ for the first person basic present tense construc-tions[2] and འདུག or ཡོད་རེད་ for the second and third persons. The rule governing the use of auxiliaries in questions is consistent with what you have learned about the future tense; that is to say, when asking a question, one uses the auxiliary verb that will be employed in answering the question. Thus, for the basic present one uses ཡོད་པས་ to ask a question that will be answered in the first person, as in ཁྱེད་རང་ཕྱག་ལས་གནང་གི་ཡོད་པས། ("Do you work?" h),[3] and one uses འདུག་གས་ or ཡོད་རེད་པས་ to ask a question that will be answered in the third person, as in ཁོང་གིས་ཕྱག་ལས་གནང་གི་འདུག་གས་ or ཁོང་གིས་ཕྱག་ལས་གནང་གི་ཡོད་རེད་པས། ("Does she work?" h). Just as we have seen that singular and plural verb endings do not differ for the future, so they do not differ for the present.

PRESENT TENSE: ALTERNATIVE FORMS

Just as the future has alternative verb forms, so too does the present. They are illustrated in

---

[1] If one is asking a fellow member of the group, one also could say ང་རང་ཚོ་ལས་ཀ་བྱེད་ཀྱི་ཡོད་པས།.

[2] As will be seen in the next section, first person alternative present tense constructions use ཡོད་རེད་.

[3] As will be seen in the next section, first person alternative present tense question constructions use ཡོད་རེད་ པས་.

the charts below. As with the future, the alternative forms are of three types:

1   changing auxiliary verbs in the first person singular and plural to de-emphasize intentionality.

2   changing from non-honorific to honorific verbs in the first person plural to honor the other members of your esteemed group.

3   changing from honorific to non-honorific pronouns and verbs in the second and third person singular and plural to speak in a common manner.

ALTERNATIVE PRESENT: DE-EMPHASIZING FIRST PERSON INTENTIONALITY

In the first person future tense, Tibetans often use the third person auxiliary verb ending གི་ རེད་ to de-emphasize the intentionality of the first person agent, as in ང་རྒྱ་གར་ལ་འགྲོ་གི་རེད། ("I will go to India"). Similarly, in the present tense they frequently use the third person auxiliary verb ending གི་ཡོད་རེད་ to de-emphasize the first-person agent, as in ངས་ཤེས་ཀྱི་ཡོད་རེད། ("I know [it]").

Alternative Present: De-Emphasizing First Person Intentionality: Affirmative Declarative			
Singular		*Plural*	
ངས་ཤེས་ཀྱི་ཡོད་རེད།	I know/ I do know	ང་ཚོས་ཤེས་ཀྱི་ཡོད་རེད།	We know/ We do know

For drills see Unit 12.21-12.23, 12.25.

The Auxiliary Verb Ending གི་འདུག་ with Non-Intentional Verbs

The basic third person present auxiliary verb ending གི་འདུག་ is not used as widely for the alternative first person present as the basic third person future auxiliary ending གི་རེད་ is used for the alternative first person future. Rather, it is employed mostly with certain verbs for which intentionality plays little role. These verbs include:

མཐོང་	to see	གཟིགས་	to see (h)
བསམ་	to think	དགོངས་	to think (h)
དྲན་	to remember	དྲན་གནང་	to remember (h)
གོ་	to hear, to understand	གསན་	to hear, to understand (h)

ཧ་གོ་	to understand	མཁྱེན་	to understand (h)
ངོ་ཤེས་	to know someone	ངོ་མཁྱེན་	to know someone (h)
ན་	to be sick	སྐྱུང་	to be sick (h)
གཉིད་འཁུགས་	to sleep	གཟིམ་འཁུགས་	to sleep (h)
བསད་	to kill	བསད་གནང་	to kill (h)
ཤི་	to die	གྲོང་	to die (h)
དགོས་	to need	དགོས་གནང་	to need (h)
འཁྱག་	to be cold	སྐུ་བསིལ་	to be cold (h)
འགྲིག་	to be correct, to be okay	འགྲིག་གནང་	to be correct, to be okay (h)
མཐུན་	to agree	མཐུན་གནང་	to agree (h)

For drills see Unit 12.24.

In the first and third persons, the auxiliary verb ending is sometimes shortened to just གི་ or its equivalents. For drills see Unit 12.26.

ALTERNATIVE PRESENT: HONORING THE OTHER MEMBERS OF YOUR ESTEEMED GROUP

When one is in a group that includes esteemed persons, such as one's parents, teachers, ordained persons, government officials, and so forth, one can use an honorific verb form for the first person plural, since the reference of the honorific is not to oneself but to others in the group. Still, some Tibetans find it uncomfortable to refer to themselves with the honorific and so find ways to get around using honorific first-person plural constructions.

Alternative Present: Honoring Your Group: Affirmative Declarative			
Singular		*Plural*	
		ང་ཚོས་མཁྱེན་གྱི་ཡོད་རེད།	We know/ We do know (h)

Alternative Present: Honoring Your Group: Affirmative Interrogative			
Singular		*Plural*	
		ང་ཚོས་མཁྱེན་གྱི་འདུག་གས། ང་ཚོས་མཁྱེན་གྱི་ཡོད་རེད་པས།	Do we know? (h)

Second person interrogatives use first person endings because they will be answered in the first person. Similarly, first person interrogatives use second person endings because they will be answered in the second person. For drills see Unit 12.27-12.32.

ALTERNATIVE PRESENT: NON-HONORIFIC SECOND AND THIRD PERSON

Since honorifics show respect for equals, superiors, or anyone to whom you wish to show deference, they should be used in almost all situations. Therefore, a good rule of thumb is to use them in all direct address and also when speaking about someone else. Still, it is important to recognize and know how to use non-honorific forms of the second and third person (in addition to those for the first person which you normally should use) since some persons, especially those from Kham (ཁམས་) , the southeastern province of Tibet, use few or no honorifics.

Alternative Present: Non-Honorific Second and Third Person: Affirmative Declarative			
Singular		*Plural*	
ཁྱེད་རང་གིས་ཤེས་ཀྱི་འདུག ཁྱེད་རང་གིས་ཤེས་ཀྱི་ཡོད་རེད།	You know/ You do know	ཁྱེད་རང་ཚོས་ཤེས་ཀྱི་འདུག ཁྱེད་རང་ཚོས་ཤེས་ཀྱི་ཡོད་རེད།	You know/ You do know
ཁོས་ཤེས་ཀྱི་འདུག ཁོས་ཤེས་ཀྱི་ཡོད་རེད།	He knows/ He does know	ཁོ་ཚོས་ཤེས་ཀྱི་འདུག ཁོ་ཚོས་ཤེས་ཀྱི་ཡོད་རེད།	They know/ They do know
མོས་ཤེས་ཀྱི་འདུག མོས་ཤེས་ཀྱི་ཡོད་རེད།	She knows/ She does know	མོ་རང་ཚོས་ཤེས་ཀྱི་ འདུག[1] མོ་རང་ཚོས་ཤེས་ཀྱི་ཡོད་ རེད།	They know/ They do know

Alternative Present: Non-Honorific Second and Third Person: Affirmative Interrogative			
Singular		*Plural*	
ཁྱེད་རང་གིས་ཤེས་ཀྱི་ཡོད་ པས།	Do you know?	ཁྱེད་རང་ཚོས་ཤེས་ཀྱི་ ཡོད་པས།	Do you know?
ཁོས་ཤེས་ཀྱི་འདུག་གས ཁོས་ཤེས་ཀྱི་ཡོད་རེད་ པས།	Does he know?	ཁོ་ཚོས་ཤེས་ཀྱི་འདུག་ གས ཁོ་ཚོས་ཤེས་ཀྱི་ཡོད་རེད་ པས།	Do they know?
མོས་ཤེས་ཀྱི་འདུག་གས མོས་ཤེས་ཀྱི་ཡོད་རེད་ པས།	Does she know?	མོ་རང་ཚོས་ཤེས་ཀྱི་ འདུག་གས[2] མོ་རང་ཚོས་ཤེས་ཀྱི་ཡོད་ རེད་པས།	Do they know?

For drills see Unit 12.33-12.46, 12.56-12.59.

---

[1] The feminine plural pronoun མོ་རང་ཚོ་ is very rare; some Central Tibetans advocate not using it at all; in place of it they use ཁོ་ཚོ་ .

[2] The feminine plural pronoun མོ་རང་ཚོ་ is very rare; some Central Tibetans advocate not using it at all; in place of it they use ཁོ་ཚོ་ .

BASIC PRESENT NEGATIVE

For the first person, མེད་ replaces ཡོད་ ; thus, in the Unit 12 dialogue Tom says ངས་ཡག་པོ་ ཤེས་ཀྱི་མེད། ("I do not know [it] well"). In the second and third persons འདུག་ becomes མི་ འདུག་ , and ཡོད་རེད་ becomes ཡོད་མ་རེད་ .

BASIC PRESENT NEGATIVE DECLARATIVE

Basic Present: Negative Declarative			
Singular		*Plural*	
ངས་ལས་ཀ་བྱེད་ཀྱི་མེད།	I do not work/ I am not working	ང་ཚོས་ལས་ཀ་བྱེད་ཀྱི་ མེད།	We do not work/ We are not working
ཁྱེད་རང་གིས་ཕྱག་ལས་ གནང་གི་མི་འདུག། ཁྱེད་རང་གིས་ཕྱག་ལས་ གནང་གི་ཡོད་མ་རེད།	You do not work/ You are not working (h)	ཁྱེད་རང་ཚོས་ཕྱག་ལས་ གནང་གི་མི་འདུག། ཁྱེད་རང་ཚོས་ཕྱག་ལས་ གནང་གི་ཡོད་མ་རེད།	You do not work/ You are not working (h)
ཁོང་གིས་ཕྱག་ལས་གནང་ གི་མི་འདུག། ཁོང་གིས་ཕྱག་ལས་གནང་ གི་ཡོད་མ་རེད།	She/he does not work/ He/she is not working (h)	ཁོང་ཚོས་ཕྱག་ལས་གནང་ གི་མི་འདུག། ཁོང་ཚོས་ཕྱག་ལས་གནང་ གི་ཡོད་མ་རེད།	They (m/f) do not work/ They are not working (h)

For drills see Unit 13.64-13.74.

BASIC PRESENT NEGATIVE INTERROGATIVE

Basic Present: Negative Interrogative			
Singular		*Plural*	
ངས་ལས་ཀ་བྱེད་ཀྱི་མེ་ འདུག་གས། ངས་ལས་ཀ་བྱེད་ཀྱི་ཡོད་ མ་རེད་པས།	Don't I work?/ Aren't I working?	ང་ཚོས་ལས་ཀ་བྱེད་ཀྱི་མེ་ འདུག་གས།[1] ང་ཚོས་ལས་ཀ་བྱེད་ཀྱི་ ཡོད་མ་རེད་པས།	Don't we work?/ Aren't we working?
ཁྱེད་རང་གིས་ཕྱག་ལས་ གནང་གི་མེད་པས།	Don't you work?/ Aren't you working? (h)	ཁྱེད་རང་ཚོས་ཕྱག་ལས་ གནང་གི་མེད་པས།	Don't you work?/ Aren't you working? (h)
ཁོང་གིས་ཕྱག་ལས་གནང་ གི་མི་འདུག་གས། ཁོང་གིས་ཕྱག་ལས་གནང་ གི་ཡོད་མ་རེད་པས།	Doesn't she/he work?/ Isn't he/she working? (h)	ཁོང་ཚོས་ཕྱག་ལས་གནང་ གི་མི་འདུག་གས། ཁོང་ཚོས་ཕྱག་ལས་གནང་ གི་ཡོད་མ་རེད་པས།	Don't they (m/f) work?/ Aren't they working? (h)

Second person interrogatives use first person endings because they will be answered in the first person. Similarly, first person interrogatives use second person endings because they will be answered in the second person. For drills see Unit 13.75-13.79.

ALTERNATIVE PRESENT NEGATIVE

ALTERNATIVE PRESENT NEGATIVE DECLARATIVE: DE-EMPHASIZING FIRST PERSON INTENTIONALITY

In the present tense, Tibetans frequently use the third person auxiliary verb གི་ཡོད་མ་རེད་ to de-emphasize the agent, as in ངས་ཤེས་ཀྱི་ཡོད་མ་རེད། ("I do not know [it]").

---

[1] If one is asking a fellow member of the group, one also could say ང་རང་ཚོས་ལས་ཀ་བྱེད་ཀྱི་མེད་པས།.

Alternative Present: De-Emphasizing First Person Intentionality: Negative Declarative			
Singular		*Plural*	
ངས་ཤེས་ཀྱི་མི་འདུག ངས་ཤེས་ཀྱི་ཡོད་མ་རེད།	I do not know	ང་ཚོས་ཤེས་ཀྱི་ཡོད་མ་ རེད།	We do not know

For a drill see Unit 13.81.

The Auxiliary Verb གི་མི་འདུག་ with Non-Intentional Verbs

As was explained above, the basic third person present ending གི་འདུག་ is not used as widely for the alternative first person present as the basic third person future auxiliary ending གི་རེད་ is used for the alternative first person future. Rather, གི་འདུག་ is employed mostly with certain verbs for which intentionality plays little role. The same is true of the alternative first person present negative. These verbs include:

མཐོང་	to see	གཟིགས་	to see (h)
བསམ་	to think	དགོངས་	to think (h)
མཐུན་	to agree	མཐུན་གནང་	to agree (h)
དྲན་	to remember	དྲན་གནང་	to remember (h)
གོ་	to hear, to understand	གསན་	to hear, to understand (h)
ཧ་གོ་	to understand	མཁྱེན་	to understand (h)
ངོ་ཤེས་	to know someone	ངོ་མཁྱེན་	to know someone (h)
ན་	to be sick	སྙུང་	to be sick (h)
གཉིད་འཁུག་	to sleep	གཟིམ་འཁུག་	to sleep (h)
བསད་	to kill	བསད་གནང་	to kill (h)
ཤི་	to die	གྲོང་	to die (h)
འགྲིག་	to be correct, to be okay	འགྲིག་གནང་	to be correct, to be okay (h)
དགོས་	to need	དགོས་གནང་	to need (h)
འཁྱགས་	to be cold	སྐུ་བསིལ་	to be cold (h)

For drills see Unit 13.82-13.83.

ALTERNATIVE PRESENT NEGATIVE INTERROGATIVE: DE-EMPHASIZING FIRST PERSON INTENTIONALITY

Alternative Present: De-Emphasizing First Person Intentionality: Negative Interrogative			
Singular		*Plural*	
ངས་ཤེས་ཀྱི་མི་འདུག་གས། ངས་ཤེས་ཀྱི་ཡོད་མ་རེད་པས།	Don't I know?	ངས་ཤེས་ཀྱི་མི་འདུག་གས། ངས་ཤེས་ཀྱི་ཡོད་མ་རེད་པས།	Don't we know?

Just as second person interrogatives use first person endings because they will be answered in the first person, first person interrogatives use second person endings because they will be answered in the second person. For a drill see Unit 13.84.

ALTERNATIVE PRESENT NEGATIVE DECLARATIVE: HONORING THE OTHER MEMBERS OF YOUR GROUP

When one is in a group that includes esteemed persons, such as one's parents, teachers, ordained persons, government officials, and so forth, one can use an honorific verb form for the first person plural, since the reference of the honorific is not to oneself but to others in the group. Still, some Tibetans find it uncomfortable to refer to themselves with the honorific and so find ways to get around using honorific first-person plural constructions.

Alternative Present: Honoring Your Group: Negative Declarative			
Singular		*Plural*	
		ང་ཚོས་མཁྱེན་གྱི་ཡོད་མ་ རེད།	We do not know (h)

For drills see Unit 13.86, 13.88.

ALTERNATIVE PRESENT NEGATIVE INTERROGATIVE: HONORING THE OTHER MEMBERS OF YOUR GROUP

Alternative Present: Honoring Your Group: Negative Interrogative			
Singular		*Plural*	
		ང་ཚོས་མཁྱེན་གྱི་མི་འདུག་གས། ང་ཚོས་མཁྱེན་གྱི་ཡོད་མ་རེད་པས།	Don't we know? (h)

Just as second person interrogatives use first person endings because they will be answered in the first person, first person interrogatives use second person endings because they will be answered in the second person. For a drill see Unit 13.89.

ALTERNATIVE PRESENT NEGATIVE DECLARATIVE: NON-HONORIFIC SECOND AND THIRD PERSON

Since honorifics show respect for equals, superiors, or anyone to whom you wish to show deference, they should be used in almost all situations. Therefore, as was indicated earlier, a good rule of thumb is to use them in all direct address or when speaking about someone else. Still, it is important to know how to use non-honorific forms of the second and third person (in addition to those for the first person which you normally should use) since some persons, especially those from Kham (ཁམས་) , the southeastern province of Tibet, use few or no honorifics.

Alternative Present: Non-Honorific Second and Third Person: Negative Declarative			
Singular		*Plural*	
ཁྱེད་རང་གྱིས་ཤེས་ཀྱི་མེ་ འདུག། ཁྱེད་རང་གྱིས་ཤེས་ཀྱི་ཡོད་ མ་རེད།	You do not know	ཁྱེད་རང་ཚོས་ཤེས་ཀྱི་མེ་ འདུག། ཁྱེད་རང་ཚོས་ཤེས་ཀྱི་ ཡོད་མ་རེད།	You do not know
ཁོས་ཤེས་ཀྱི་མེ་འདུག། ཁོས་ཤེས་ཀྱི་ཡོད་མ་རེད།	He does not know	ཁོ་ཚོས་ཤེས་ཀྱི་མེ་འདུག། ཁོ་ཚོས་ཤེས་ཀྱི་ཡོད་མ་ རེད།	They do not know
མོས་ཤེས་ཀྱི་མེ་འདུག། མོས་ཤེས་ཀྱི་ཡོད་མ་རེད།	She does not know	མོ་རང་ཚོས་ཤེས་ཀྱི་མེ་ འདུག།[1] མོ་རང་ཚོས་ཤེས་ཀྱི་ཡོད་ མ་རེད།	They do not know

For drills see Unit 13.90-13.100.

---

[1] The feminine plural pronoun མོ་རང་ཚོ་ is very rare; some Central Tibetans advocate not using it at all; in place of it they use ཁོ་ཚོ་ .

ALTERNATIVE PRESENT NEGATIVE INTERROGATIVE: NON-HONORIFIC SECOND AND THIRD PERSON

Alternative Present: Non-Honorific Second and Third Person: Negative Interrogative			
Singular		*Plural*	
ཁྱེད་རང་གྱིས་ཤེས་ཀྱི་མེད་པས།	Don't you know?	ཁྱེད་རང་ཚོས་ཤེས་ཀྱི་མེད་པས།	Don't you know?
ཁོས་ཤེས་ཀྱི་མི་འདུག་གས།	Doesn't he know?	ཁོ་ཚོས་ཤེས་ཀྱི་མི་འདུག་གས།	Don't they know?
ཁོས་ཤེས་ཀྱི་ཡོད་མ་རེད་པས།		ཁོ་ཚོས་ཤེས་ཀྱི་ཡོད་མ་རེད་པས།	
མོས་ཤེས་ཀྱི་མི་འདུག་གས།	Doesn't she know?	མོ་རང་ཚོས་ཤེས་ཀྱི་མི་འདུག་གས།[1]	Don't they know?
མོས་ཤེས་ཀྱི་ཡོད་མ་རེད་པས།		མོ་རང་ཚོས་ཤེས་ཀྱི་ཡོད་མ་རེད་པས།	

For a drill see Unit 13.101.

PAST TENSE

In Unit 14, Ḍröl-<u>ma</u>, having learned that Susan is studying Tibetan, asks Tom ཁོང་འདིར་ག་དུས་ཕེབས་པ་རེད། ("When did she come here?" h). Tom answers ཟླ་བ་གསུམ་གྱི་སྔོན་ལ་ཕེབས་པ་རེད། ("She came three months ago" h). Their exchange introduces the form and use of the past tense. As was explained above, the future, present, and past tenses of Tibetan verbs are indicated through the use of different auxiliary verb endings and through changes in the form of the main verb. However, the form of the main verb frequently does not vary from tense to tense, and many of the changes that the main verb does undergo either cannot be

---

[1] The feminine plural pronoun མོ་རང་ཚོ་ is very rare; some Central Tibetans advocate not using it at all; in place of it they use ཁོ་ཚོ་.

heard, can be heard only with difficulty, or are not widely used in colloquial Tibetan. Therefore, it is principally the auxiliary verb ending that indicates the tense to the listener. As was explained above, the future tense uses the auxiliary verb endings གི་ཡིན་ and གི་རེད་, while the present tense uses the auxiliary verb endings གི་ཡོད་, གི་འདུག་, and གི་ཡོད་རེད་. The past tense uses པ་ཡིན་, སོང་, པ་རེད་, and བྱུང་. First we will consider the basic past verb forms; then we will examine the alternative ones.

PAST TENSE: BASIC FORMS

To say, "I worked," one uses the basic first person auxiliary verb ending པ་ཡིན་, and combines it with the past tense form of a main verb, for example བྱས་ ("did"). Thus, ངས་ལས་ཀ་ བྱས་པ་ཡིན། ("I worked", "I was working", or "I did work") is an example of the basic first person past tense form. Similarly, because the question "Did you work?" will be answered in the first person, one uses the auxiliary པ་ཡིན་ with the question particle པས་ to form a second person interrogative construction, as in ཁྱེད་རང་གིས་ཕྱག་ལས་གནང་པ་ཡིན་པས། ("Did you work?" or "Were you working?" h). For first person past negative declarative statements, one merely says ངས་ལས་ཀ་མ་བྱས། ("I did not work," or "I was not working").[1]

Second person expressions use the auxiliary verb སོང་ (except, as we have just seen, for those occasions when one is posing a question that will be answered in the first person); for example, ཁྱེད་རང་གིས་ཕྱག་ལས་གནང་སོང་། ("You worked", "You were working", or "You did work" h). Third person declarative statements are formed the same way; thus ཁོང་གིས་ ཕྱག་ལས་གནང་སོང་། ("She/he worked", "She/he was working", or "She/he did work" h). Hence, for both the second and third person one joins the auxiliary verb སོང་ to a main verb such as གནང་ ("did" h) to make the past tense verb form, in this case གནང་སོང་. If one wishes to ask a question about a third person, one adds the interrogative particle ངས་ at the end, as in ཁོང་གིས་ཕྱག་ལས་གནང་སོང་ངས། ("Did he/she work?" or "Was he/she working?" h). The negative for both the second and the third persons is formed by adding མ་ before སོང་, as in ཁོང་གིས་ཕྱག་ལས་གནང་མ་སོང་། ("She/he did not work" or "She/he was not working" h).

In sum, the use of auxiliary verbs in declarative statements is simple: use པ་ཡིན་ for the first person and སོང་ for the second and third persons. Just as singular and plural verb endings do not differ in the future or present tenses, so they do not differ in the past tense.

---

[1] One does not say ངས་ལས་ཀ་བྱས་པ་མེན།.

Basic Past: Affirmative Declarative			
Singular		*Plural*	
ངས་ལས་ཀ་བྱས་པ་ཨིན།	I worked/ I was working/ I did work	ང་ཚོས་ལས་ཀ་བྱས་པ་ཨིན།	We worked/ We were working/ We did work
ཁྱེད་རང་གིས་ཕྱག་ལས་གནང་སོང་།	You worked/ You were working/ You did work (h)	ཁྱེད་རང་ཚོས་ཕྱག་ལས་གནང་སོང་།	You worked/ You were working/ You did work (h)
ཁོང་གིས་ཕྱག་ལས་གནང་སོང་།	She/he worked/ He/she was working/ She/he did work (h)	ཁོང་ཚོས་ཕྱག་ལས་གནང་སོང་།	They (m/f) worked/ They were working/ They did work (h)

For drills see Unit 14.10-14.13, 14.17-14.18, 14.22, 14.24, 14.27.

Basic Past: Negative Declarative			
Singular		*Plural*	
ངས་ལས་ཀ་མ་བྱས།	I did not work/ I was not working	ང་ཚོས་ལས་ཀ་མ་བྱས།	We did not work/ We were not working
ཁྱེད་རང་གིས་ཕྱག་ལས་གནང་མ་སོང་།	You did not work/ You were not working (h)	ཁྱེད་རང་ཚོས་ཕྱག་ལས་གནང་མ་སོང་།	You did not work/ You were not working (h)
ཁོང་གིས་ཕྱག་ལས་གནང་མ་སོང་།	She/he did not work/ He/she was not working (h)	ཁོང་ཚོས་ཕྱག་ལས་གནང་མ་སོང་།	They (m/f) did not work/ They were not working (h)

For drills see Unit 14.14, 14.19, 14.23.

Interrogatives: The rule governing the use of auxiliary verbs in questions is consistent with what you learned about the future and present tenses; that is to say, when asking a question, one uses the auxiliary verb that will be employed in the answer. Thus, one uses པ་ཨིན་པས་ to ask a question that will be answered in the first person, as in ཁྱེད་རང་གིས་ཕྱག་ལས་གནང་པ་ཨིན་པས། ("Did you work" or "Were you working?" h). Just as the second person future interrogative verb ending is frequently contracted from གི་ཨིན་པས་ to གས་, the second person interrogative past verb ending is frequently contracted from པ་ཨིན་པས་ to པས་. For example, ཁྱེད་རང་གིས་ཕྱག་ལས་གནང་པས། is often used in place of ཁྱེད་རང་གིས་ཕྱག་ལས་གནང་པ་ཨིན་པས།. Like the future tense, second person interrogative past tense constructions with interrogative particles have a full and a contracted form. For example, "Where did you work?" (h) can be expressed in Tibetan either as ཁྱེད་རང་གིས་ཕྱག་ལས་ག་པར་གནང་པ་ཡིན་པ། or as ཁྱེད་རང་གིས་ཕྱག་ལས་ག་པར་གནང་པ།. One uses སོང་ངས་ to ask a question that will be answered in the third person, as in ཁོང་གིས་ཕྱག་ལས་གནང་སོང་ངས། ("Did he/she work?" or "Was he/she working?" h). For questions that are asked in the first person, such as "Did I go there?", one says ང་ཕ་གིར་ཕྱིན་སོང་ངས། because the question will be answered in the second person, as in ཁྱེད་རང་ཕ་གིར་ཕེབས་སོང་། ("You went there" h).

Basic Past: Affirmative Interrogative			
Singular		*Plural*	
ངས་ལས་ཀ་བྱས་སོང་ངས།	Did I work?/ Was I working?	ང་ཚོས་ལས་ཀ་བྱས་སོང་ངས།[1]	Did we work?/ Were we working?
ཁྱེད་རང་གིས་ཕྱག་ལས་གནང་པ་ཡིན་པས། ཁྱེད་རང་གིས་ཕྱག་ལས་གནང་པས།	Did you work?/ Were you working? (h)	ཁྱེད་རང་ཚོས་ཕྱག་ལས་གནང་པ་ཡིན་པས། ཁྱེད་རང་ཚོས་ཕྱག་ལས་གནང་པས།	Did you work?/ Were you working? (h)
ཁོང་གིས་ཕྱག་ལས་གནང་སོང་ངས།	Did she/he work?/ Was she/he working? (h)	ཁོང་ཚོས་ཕྱག་ལས་གནང་སོང་ངས།	Did they (m/f) work?/ Were they working? (h)

For drills see Unit 14.15, 14.20, 14.25-14.26.

First person and third person negative interrogative constructions are formed by adding མ་ before the auxiliary སོང་ངས་, as in ཁོང་གིས་ཕྱག་ལས་གནང་མ་སོང་ངས། ("Didn't she/he work?" or "Wasn't she/he working?" h). Second person negative interrogative past constructions are formed by changing the auxiliary verb ending from ཡིན་པས་ to མིན་པས་. For instance, "Didn't you work?" or "Weren't you working?" (h) is rendered in Tibetan as ཁྱེད་རང་གིས་ཕྱག་ལས་གནང་པ་མིན་པས།. The contracted form is constructed by adding མ་ before the main verb and the question particle, as in ཁྱེད་རང་གིས་ཕྱག་ལས་མ་གནང་པས། ("Didn't you work?" or "Weren't you working?" h).

---

[1] If one is asking a fellow member of the group, one also could say ང་རང་ཚོས་ལས་ཀ་བྱས་པ་ཡིན་པས། or ང་རང་ཚོས་ལས་ཀ་བྱས་པས།.

Basic Past: Negative Interrogative			
Singular		*Plural*	
ངས་ལས་ཀ་བྱས་མ་སོང་ངས།	Didn't I work?/ Wasn't I working?	ང་ཚོས་ལས་ཀ་བྱས་མ་སོང་ངས།[1]	Didn't we work?/ Weren't we working?
ཁྱེད་རང་གིས་ཕྱག་ལས་མ་གནང་པས།	Didn't you work?/ Weren't you working? (h)	ཁྱེད་རང་ཚོས་ཕྱག་ལས་མ་གནང་པས།	Didn't you work?/ Weren't you working? (h)
ཁོང་གིས་ཕྱག་ལས་གནང་མ་སོང་ངས།	Didn't she/he work?/ Wasn't she/he working? (h)	ཁོང་ཚོས་ཕྱག་ལས་གནང་མ་སོང་ངས།	Didn't they (m/f) work?/ Weren't they working? (h)

For drills on basic past forms see Unit 14.16, 14.21.

PAST TENSE: ALTERNATIVE FORMS

Just as the future and present tenses have alternative verb forms, so too does the past tense. The charts below illustrate the past alternative verb forms. The alternative forms are of four types:

1   changing auxiliary verbs in the first person singular and plural to de-emphasize intentionality.

2   changing from non-honorific to honorific verbs in the first person plural to honor the other members of your esteemed group.

3   changing from honorific to non-honorific pronouns and verbs in the second and third person singular and plural to speak in a common manner.

4   changing to a less common but frequently used form of auxiliary verb in the second and third persons singular and plural— སོང་ to པ་རེད་.

ALTERNATIVE PAST: DE-EMPHASIZING FIRST PERSON INTENTIONALITY

As we have seen, for first person future and present tense constructions, Tibetans often use the third person auxiliary verb forms—གི་རེད་ for the future and གི་ཡོད་རེད་ for the present—to de-emphasize the intentionality of the first person agent. For example, one can say ང་བལ་ ཡུལ་ལ་འགྲོ་གི་རེད། ("I will go to Nepal") and ང་རྒྱ་གར་ལ་འགྲོ་གི་ཡོད་རེད། ("I am going to India"). Similarly, in the past tense Tibetans often use the third person auxiliary verb ending པ་རེད་

---

[1] If one is asking a fellow member of the group, one also could say ང་རང་ཚོས་ལས་ཀ་མ་བྱས་པས།.

to de-emphasize the first person agent, as in ངས་ལས་ཀ་བྱས་པ་རེད། ("I worked," "I did work," or "I was working").

Alternative Past: De-Emphasizing First Person Intentionality: Affirmative Declarative			
Singular		*Plural*	
ངས་ལས་ཀ་བྱས་པ་རེད།	I worked/ I was working/ I did work	ང་ཚོས་ལས་ཀ་བྱས་པ་ རེད།	We worked/ We were working/ We did work

For a drill see Unit 14.28.

Interrogatives. The corresponding interrogative construction is framed in the second person but uses the third person auxiliary endings since it will be answered in that form:

Singular		*Plural*	
ཁྱེད་རང་གིས་ཕྱག་ལས་ གནང་པ་རེད་པས། ཁྱེད་རང་གིས་ལས་ཀ་བྱས་ པ་རེད་པས།	Did you work?/ Were you working? (h)	ཁྱེད་རང་ཚོས་ཕྱག་ལས་ གནང་པ་རེད་པས། ཁྱེད་རང་ཚོས་ལས་ཀ་ བྱས་པ་རེད་པས།	Did you work?/ Were you working?(h)

For a drill see Unit 14.29.

Alternative Past: De-Emphasizing First Person Intentionality: Negative Declarative			
Singular		*Plural*	
ངས་ལས་ཀ་མ་བྱས་པ་ རེད།	I did not work/ I was not working	ང་ཚོས་ལས་ཀ་མ་བྱས་པ་ རེད།	We did not work/ We were not working

Since this construction is drilled in this book in question and answer format, it is necessary first to understand that the corresponding interrogative construction is framed in the second person using the third person auxiliary endings since it will be answered in that form:

Singular		*Plural*	
ཁྱེད་རང་གིས་ཕྱག་ལས་མ་ གནང་པ་རེད་པས། ཁྱེད་རང་གིས་ལས་ཀ་མ་ བྱས་པ་རེད་པས།	Didn't you work?/ Weren't you working? (h)	ཁྱེད་རང་ཚོས་ཕྱག་ལས་ མ་གནང་པ་རེད་པས། ཁྱེད་རང་ཚོས་ལས་ཀ་མ་ བྱས་པ་རེད་པས།	Didn't you work?/ Weren't you working? (h)

For a drill see Unit 14.30.

Past constructions with ཤུང་

As we have seen, in the present tense one uses the third person present ending གི་འདུག for the first person with certain verbs for which intentionality plays little role. Similarly, in the past tense, with most of these same verbs one uses སོང་, པ་རེད་, or ཤུང་ rather than པ་ཡིན་. These verbs include:

ཤེས་	to know	མཁྱེན་	to know (h)
མཐོང་	to see	གཟིགས་	to see (h)
བསམ་	to think	དགོངས་	to think (h)
མཐུན་	to agree	མཐུན་གནང་	to agree (h)
དྲན་	to remember	དྲན་གནང་	to remember (h)
གོ	to hear, to understand	གསན་	to hear, to understand (h)
ཏུ་གོ	to understand	མཁྱེན་	to understand (h)
ངོ་ཤེས་	to know someone	ངོ་མཁྱེན་	to know someone (h)
གཉིད་འཁགས་	to sleep	གཟིམ་འཁགས་	to sleep (h)
བསད་	to kill	བསད་གནང་	to kill (h)
ཤི	to die	གྲོང་	to die (h)
འགྲིགས་	to be correct, to be okay	འགྲིགས་གནང་	to be correct, to be okay (h)
དགོས་	to need	དགོས་གནང་	to need (h)
འཁྱགས་	to be cold	སྐུ་བསིལ་	to be cold (h)

For drills see Unit 14.31-14.32.

ALTERNATIVE PAST: HONORING THE OTHER MEMBERS OF YOUR ESTEEMED GROUP

When one is in a group that includes esteemed persons, such as one's parents, teachers, ordained persons, government officials, and so forth, one can use an honorific verb form for the first person plural, since the reference of the honorific is not to oneself but to others in the group. Still, some Tibetans find it uncomfortable to refer to themselves with the honorific and so find ways to get around using honorific first-person plural constructions.

Alternative Past: Honoring Your Group: Affirmative Declarative			
Singular		*Plural*	
		ང་ཚོས་ཕྱག་ལས་གནང་པ་ རེད།	We worked/ We were working/ We did work (h)

For drills see Unit 14.33-14.34.

Alternative Past: Honoring Your Group: Negative Declarative			
Singular		*Plural*	
		ང་ཚོས་ཕྱག་ལས་མ་ གནང་པ་རེད།	We did not work/ We were not working (h)

For a drill see Unit 14.35.

Alternative Past: Honoring Your Group: Affirmative Interrogative			
Singular		*Plural*	
		ང་ཚོས་ཕྱག་ལས་གནང་ སོང་ངས།[1] ང་ཚོས་ཕྱག་ལས་གནང་པ་ རེད་པས།	Did we work?/ Were we working? (h)

Just as second person interrogative constructions use first person endings because they will be answered in the first person, first person interrogative constructions use second person endings because they will be answered in the second person. For drills see Unit 14.36-14.37.

[1] To a fellow member of one's group, one also could say ང་རང་ཚོས་ཕྱག་ལས་གནང་པ་ཡིན་པས། or ང་རང་ཚོས་ཕྱག་ལས་ གནང་པས། .

Alternative Past: Honoring Your Group: Negative Interrogative		
Singular		*Plural*
		ང་ཚོས་ཕྱག་ལས་གནང་ མ་སོང་ངས།[1] ང་ཚོས་ཕྱག་ལས་མ་ གནང་པ་རེད་པས།	Didn't we work?/ Weren't we working? (h)

Just as second person interrogative constructions use first person endings because they will be answered in the first person, first person interrogative constructions use second person endings because they will be answered in the second person. For drills see Unit 14.38-14.39.

ALTERNATIVE PAST: NON-HONORIFIC SECOND AND THIRD PERSON

Since honorifics show respect for equals, superiors, or anyone to whom you wish to show deference, they should be used in almost all situations. Therefore, as was indicated earlier, a good rule of thumb is to use them in all direct address or when speaking about someone else. Still, it is important to know how to use non-honorific forms of the second and third person (in addition to those for the first person which you normally should use) since some persons, especially those from Kam (ཁམས་), the southeastern province of Tibet, use few or no honorifics.

Alternative Past: Non-Honorific Second and Third Person: Affirmative Declarative			
Singular		*Plural*	
ཁྱེད་རང་གིས་ལས་ཀ་བྱས་ སོང་།	You worked/ You were working/ You did work	ཁྱེད་རང་ཚོས་ལས་ཀ་ བྱས་སོང་།	You worked/ You were working/ You did work
ཁོས་ལས་ཀ་བྱས་སོང་།	He worked/ He was working/ He did work	ཁོ་ཚོས་ལས་ཀ་བྱས་སོང་།	They worked/ They were working/ They did work
མོས་ལས་ཀ་བྱས་སོང་།	She worked/ She was working/ She did work	མོ་རང་ཚོས་ལས་ཀ་བྱས་ སོང་།[2]	They worked/ They were working/ They did work

For drills see Unit 14.40.

---

[1] To a fellow member of one's group, one also could say ང་རང་ཚོས་ཕྱག་ལས་མ་གནང་པས། .

[2] The feminine plural pronoun མོ་རང་ཚོ་ is very rare; some Central Tibetans advocate not using it at all; in place of it they use ཁོ་ཚོ་ .

Alternative Past: Non-Honorific Second and Third Person: Negative Declarative			
Singular		*Plural*	
ཁྱེད་རང་གིས་ལས་ཀ་བྱས་མ་སོང་།	You did not work/ You were not working	ཁྱེད་རང་ཚོས་ལས་ཀ་བྱས་མ་སོང་།	You did not work/ You were not working
ཁོས་ལས་ཀ་བྱས་མ་སོང་།	He did not work/ He was not working	ཁོ་ཚོས་ལས་ཀ་བྱས་མ་སོང་།	They did not work/ They were not working
མོས་ལས་ཀ་བྱས་མ་སོང་།	She did not work/ She was not working	མོ་རང་ཚོས་ལས་ཀ་བྱས་མ་སོང་།[1]	They did not work/ They were not working

For a drill see Unit 14.41.

Alternative Past: Non-Honorific Second and Third Person: Affirmative Interrogative			
Singular		*Plural*	
ཁྱེད་རང་གིས་ལས་ཀ་བྱས་པ་ཡིན་པས། ཁྱེད་རང་གིས་ལས་ཀ་བྱས་པས།	Did you work?/ Were you working?	ཁྱེད་རང་ཚོས་ལས་ཀ་བྱས་པ་ཡིན་པས། ཁྱེད་རང་ཚོས་ལས་ཀ་བྱས་པས།	Did you work?/ Were you working?
ཁོས་ལས་ཀ་བྱས་སོང་ངས།	Did he work?/ Was he working?	ཁོ་ཚོས་ལས་ཀ་བྱས་སོང་ངས།	Did they work?/ Were they working?
མོས་ལས་ཀ་བྱས་སོང་ངས།	Did she work?/ Was she working?	མོ་རང་ཚོས་ལས་ཀ་བྱས་སོང་ངས།[2]	Did they work?/ Were they working?

For a drill see Unit 14.42.

---

[1] The feminine plural pronoun མོ་རང་ཚོ་ is very rare; some Central Tibetans advocate not using it at all; in place of it they use ཁོ་ཚོ་.

[2] The feminine plural pronoun མོ་རང་ཚོ་ is very rare; some Central Tibetans advocate not using it at all; in place of it they use ཁོ་ཚོ་.

Alternative Past: Non-Honorific Second and Third Person: Negative Interrogative			
Singular		*Plural*	
ཁྱོད་རང་གིས་ལས་ཀ་མ་ བྱས་པས།	Didn't you work?/ Weren't you working?	ཁྱོད་རང་ཚོས་ལས་ཀ་མ་ བྱས་པས།	Didn't you work?/ Weren't you working?
ཁོས་ལས་ཀ་བྱས་མ་སོང་ ངས།	Didn't he work?/ Wasn't he working?	ཁོ་ཚོས་ལས་ཀ་བྱས་མ་ སོང་ངས།	Didn't they work?/ Weren't they working?
མོས་ལས་ཀ་བྱས་མ་སོང་ ངས།	Didn't she work?/ Wasn't she working?	མོ་རང་ཚོས་ལས་ཀ་བྱས་ མ་སོང་ངས།[1]	Didn't they work?/ Weren't they working?

For a drill see Unit 14.43.

CHANGING AUXILIARY VERB FROM སོང་ TO པ་རེད་ IN THE SECOND AND THIRD PERSON SINGULAR AND PLURAL

The auxiliary verb ending པ་རེད་ is frequently used in place of སོང་ in the second and third person singular and plural. པ་རེད་ often indicates an on-going action that occurred in the past.

---

[1] The feminine plural pronoun མོ་རང་ཚོ་ is very rare; some Central Tibetans advocate not using it at all; in

Alternative Past: Changing སོང་ to པ་རེད་ in Second and Third Persons: Affirmative Declarative			
Singular		*Plural*	
ཁྱེད་རང་གིས་ཕྱག་ལས་ གནང་པ་རེད། ཁྱེད་རང་གིས་ལས་ཀ་བྱས་ པ་རེད།	You worked/ You were working/ You did work (h)	ཁྱེད་རང་ཚོས་ཕྱག་ལས་ གནང་པ་རེད། ཁྱེད་རང་ཚོས་ལས་ཀ་ བྱས་པ་རེད།	You worked/ You were working/ You did work (h)
ཁོང་གིས་ཕྱག་ལས་གནང་ པ་རེད། ཁོས་ལས་ཀ་བྱས་པ་རེད།	He worked/ He was working/ He did work (h)	ཁོང་ཚོས་ཕྱག་ལས་གནང་ པ་རེད། ཁོ་ཚོས་ལས་ཀ་བྱས་པ་ རེད།	They worked/ They were working/ They did work (h)
ཁོང་གིས་ཕྱག་ལས་གནང་ པ་རེད། མོས་ལས་ཀ་བྱས་པ་རེད།	She worked/ She was working/ She did work (h)	ཁོང་ཚོས་ཕྱག་ལས་གནང་ པ་རེད། མོ་རང་ཚོས་ལས་ཀ་བྱས་ པ་རེད།	They worked/ They were working/ They did work (h)

For a drill see Unit 14.44.

place of it they use ཁ་ཚོ་ .

Alternative Past: Changing ཤོང་ to པ་རེད་ in Second and Third Person: Negative Declarative			
Singular		*Plural*	
ཁྱེད་རང་གིས་ཕྱག་ལས་མ་གནང་པ་རེད། ཁྱེད་རང་གིས་ལས་ཀ་མ་བྱས་པ་རེད།	You did not work/ You were not working (h)	ཁྱེད་རང་ཚོས་ཕྱག་ལས་མ་གནང་པ་རེད། ཁྱེད་རང་ཚོས་ལས་ཀ་མ་བྱས་པ་རེད།	You did not work/ You were not working (h)
ཁོང་གིས་ཕྱག་ལས་མ་གནང་པ་རེད། ཁོས་ལས་ཀ་མ་བྱས་པ་རེད།	He did not work/ He was not working (h)	ཁོང་ཚོས་ཕྱག་ལས་མ་གནང་པ་རེད། ཁོ་ཚོས་ལས་ཀ་མ་བྱས་པ་རེད།	They did not work/ They were not working (h)
ཁོང་གིས་ཕྱག་ལས་མ་གནང་པ་རེད། མོས་ལས་ཀ་མ་བྱས་པ་རེད།	She did not work/ She was not working (h)	ཁོང་ཚོས་ཕྱག་ལས་མ་གནང་པ་རེད། མོ་རང་ཚོས་ལས་ཀ་མ་བྱས་པ་རེད།	They did not work/ They were not working (h)

For a drill see Unit 14.45.

Alternative Past: Changing ཤོང་ to པ་རེད་ in the Third Person: Affirmative Interrogative			
Singular		*Plural*	
ཁོང་གིས་ཕྱག་ལས་གནང་པ་རེད་པས། ཁོས་ལས་ཀ་བྱས་པ་རེད་པས།	Did he work?/ Was he working? (h)	ཁོང་ཚོས་ཕྱག་ལས་གནང་པ་རེད་པས། ཁོ་ཚོས་ལས་ཀ་བྱས་པ་རེད་པས།	Did they work?/ Were they working? (h)
ཁོང་གིས་ཕྱག་ལས་གནང་པ་རེད་པས། མོས་ལས་ཀ་བྱས་པ་རེད་པས།	Did she work?/ Was she working? (h)	ཁོང་ཚོས་ཕྱག་ལས་གནང་པ་རེད་པས། མོ་རང་ཚོས་ལས་ཀ་བྱས་པ་རེད་པས།	Did they work?/ Were they working? (h)

For drills see Unit 14.46-14.47.

Since the first person interrogative form accords with the second and third person declarative form, there is also a first person interrogative:

Alternative Past: Changing སོང་ to པ་རེད་ in First Person Affirmative Interrogative			
Singular		*Plural*	
ངས་ལས་ཀ་བྱས་པ་རེད་ པས།	Did I work?/ Was I working?	ང་ཚོས་ལས་ཀ་བྱས་པ་ རེད་པས།	Did we work?/ Were we working?

For a drill see Unit 14.48.

Alternative Past: Changing སོང་ to པ་རེད་ in the Third Person: Negative Interrogative			
Singular		*Plural*	
ཁོང་གིས་ཕྱག་ལས་མ་ གནང་པ་རེད་པས། ཁོས་ལས་ཀ་མ་བྱས་པ་ རེད་པས།	Didn't he work?/ Wasn't he working? (h)	ཁོང་ཚོས་ཕྱག་ལས་མ་ གནང་པ་རེད་པས། ཁོ་ཚོས་ལས་ཀ་མ་བྱས་པ་ རེད་པས།	Didn't they work?/ Weren't they working? (h)
ཁོང་གིས་ཕྱག་ལས་མ་ གནང་པ་རེད་པས། མོས་ལས་ཀ་མ་བྱས་པ་ རེད་པས།	Didn't she work?/ Wasn't she working? (h)	ཁོང་ཚོས་ཕྱག་ལས་མ་ གནང་པ་རེད་པས། མོ་རང་ཚོས་ལས་ཀ་མ་ བྱས་པ་རེད་པས།	Didn't they work?/ Weren't they working? (h)

For drills see Unit 14.49-14.50.

Since the first person negative interrogative form accords with the second and third person declarative form, there is also a first person negative interrogative:

Alternative Past: Changing སོང་ to པ་རེད་ in First Person Negative Interrogative			
Singular		*Plural*	
ངས་ལས་ཀ་མ་བྱས་པ་ རེད་པས།	Didn't I work?/ Wasn't I working?	ང་ཚོས་ལས་ཀ་མ་བྱས་པ་ རེད་པས།	Didn't we work?/ Weren't we working?

For a drill see Unit 14.51.

CHANGING TENSES

The following chart lists the three tenses of all verbs in this book, arranged Unit by Unit.

Future	Present	Past	English
Unit 6			
འགྲོ་	འགྲོ་	ཕྱིན་	to go
ཕེབས་	ཕེབས་	ཕེབས་	to go (h)
Unit 7			
བཟའ་	ཟ་	བཟས་	to eat
མཆོད་	མཆོད་	མཆོད་	to eat (h)
བཏུང་	འཐུང་	བཏུངས་	to drink
མཆོད་	མཆོད་	མཆོད་	to drink (h)
བཀླག	ཀློག	བཀླགས་	to read
ཕྱགས་ཀློག་གནང་	ཕྱགས་ཀློག་གནང་	ཕྱགས་ཀློག་གནང་	to read (h)
ཉོ་	ཉོ་	ཉོས་	to buy
གཟིགས་	གཟིགས་	གཟིགས་	to buy (h)
Unit 10			
བསྡད་	སྡོད་	བསྡད་	to sit, to stay
བཞུགས་	བཞུགས་	བཞུགས་	to sit, to stay (h)
བསྲེག[1]	སྲེག	བསྲེགས་	to roast
བསྲེགས་གནང་	བསྲེགས་གནང་	བསྲེགས་གནང་	to roast (h)
རྔད་བཙོས་བརྒྱབ	རྔད་བཙོས་རྒྱབ་	རྔད་བཙོས་བརྒྱབས་	to steam
རྔད་བཙོས་བསྐྱོན་	རྔད་བཙོས་སྐྱོན་	རྔད་བཙོས་བསྐྱོནད་	to steam (h)
བརྔོ་	རྔོ་	བརྔོས་	to fry (foods), to parch (barley)
བརྔོས་གནང་	བརྔོས་གནང་	བརྔོས་གནང་	to fry (foods), to parch (barley) (h)
བཟོ་	བཟོ་	བཟོས་	to make, to prepare
བཟོས་གནང་	བཟོས་གནང་	བཟོས་གནང་	to make, to prepare (h)
བཙོང་	འཚོང་	བཙོངས་	to sell

---

[1] Pronounced ḍa'.

ཚོང་བསྒྱུར	ཚོང་སྒྱུར	ཚོང་བསྒྱུརད	to sell (h)
Unit 11			
བྱ	བྱེད	བྱས	to do
གནང་	གནང་	གནང་	to do (h)
སློབ་སྦྱོང་བྱ	སློབ་སྦྱོང་བྱེད	སློབ་སྦྱོང་བྱས	to study
སློབ་སྦྱོང་གནང་	སློབ་སྦྱོང་གནང་	སློབ་སྦྱོང་གནང་	to study (h)
ཡོང་	ཡོང་	ཡོང་	to come
བྲི	འབྲི	བྲིས	to write, to paint, to draw
བྲིས་གནང་	བྲིས་གནང་	བྲིས་གནང་	to write, to paint, to draw (h)
བསླེབ	སླེབ	བསླེབས	to arrive
འབྱོར	འབྱོར	འབྱོརད	to arrive
འབྱོར་གནང་	འབྱོར་གནང་	འབྱོར་གནང་	to arrive (h)
ཕེབས་འབྱོར་གནང་	ཕེབས་འབྱོར་གནང་	ཕེབས་འབྱོར་གནང་	to arrive (h)
Unit 12			
ཁ་པར་གཏང་	ཁ་པར་གཏོང་	ཁ་པར་བཏང་	to telephone
ཞལ་པར་བཏང་གནང་	ཞལ་པར་བཏང་གནང་	ཞལ་པར་བཏང་གནང་	to telephone (h)
རླུགས་པ་བརྒྱབ	རླུགས་པ་རྒྱབ	རླུགས་པ་བརྒྱབས	to be windy
ཆར་པ་གཏང་	ཆར་པ་གཏོང་	ཆར་པ་བཏང་	to rain
སྤྱར	སྤྱོར	སྤྱརད	to ignite, to turn on
སྤྱར་གནང་	སྤྱར་གནང་	སྤྱར་གནང་	to ignite, to turn on (h)
གསད་	གསོད་	བསད་	to kill, to turn off
བསད་གནང་	བསད་གནང་	བསད་གནང་	to kill, to turn off (h)
མོ་ཊར་གཏང་	མོ་ཊར་གཏོང་	མོ་ཊར་བཏང་	to drive a car
མོ་ཊར་བཏང་གནང་	མོ་ཊར་གཏོང་གནང་	མོ་ཊར་བཏང་གནང་	to drive a car (h)
རྨི་ལམ་གཏང་	རྨི་ལམ་གཏོང་	རྨི་ལམ་བཏང་	to dream
རྨི་ལམ་བཏང་གནང་	རྨི་ལམ་བཏང་གནང་	རྨི་ལམ་བཏང་གནང་	to dream (h)

ལས་ཀ་བྱུ་	ལས་ཀ་བྱེད་	ལས་ཀ་བྱུས་	to work
ཕྱག་ལས་གནང་	ཕྱག་ལས་གནང་	ཕྱག་ལས་གནང་	to work (h)
བརྒྱབ་	རྒྱབ་	བརྒྱབས་	to build, to make, to put
བསྐྲུན་	སྐྲུན་	བསྐྲུནད་	to build, to make, to put (h)
ངལ་གསོ་བརྒྱབ་	ངལ་གསོ་རྒྱབ་	ངལ་གསོ་བརྒྱབས་	to rest
ངལ་གསོ་བསྐྲུན་	ངལ་གསོ་སྐྲུན་	ངལ་གསོ་བསྐྲུནད་	to rest (h)
གཡར་	གཡར་	གཡར་ད་	to borrow, to lend
གཡར་གནང་	གཡར་གནང་	གཡར་གནང་	to borrow, to lend (h)
ཤེས་	ཤེས་	ཤེས་	to know
མཁྱེན་	མཁྱེན་	མཁྱེནད་	to know (h)
མཐོང་	མཐོང་	མཐོང་	to see
གཟིགས་	གཟིགས་	གཟིགས་	to see (h)
ངོ་ཤེས་	ངོ་ཤེས་	ངོ་ཤེས་	to know someone
ངོ་མཁྱེན་	ངོ་མཁྱེན་	ངོ་མཁྱེནད་	to know someone (h)
བསམ་	སེམས་	བསམས་	to think
དགོངས་	དགོངས་	དགོངས་	to think (h)
དགོས་	དགོས་	དགོས་	to need, to want
དགོས་གནང་	དགོས་གནང་	དགོས་གནང་	to need, to want (h)
མཐུན་	མཐུན་	མཐུནད་	to agree
མཐུན་གནང་	མཐུན་གནང་	མཐུན་གནང་	to agree (h)
འགྲིག་	འགྲིག་	འགྲིགས་	to be correct, to be okay
དྲན་	དྲན་	དྲནད་	to remember
དྲན་གནང་	དྲན་གནང་	དྲནད་གནང་	to remember (h)
འཁྱག་	འཁྱག་	འཁྱགས་	to feel cold
སྐུ་བསིལ་	སྐུ་བསིལ་	སྐུ་བསིལ་	to feel cold (h)

ན་	ན་	ན་	to be sick
བསྡུང་	སྡུང་	བསྡུངས་	to be sick (h)
ཆམས་པ་བརྒྱབ་	ཆམས་པ་རྒྱབ་	ཆམས་པ་བརྒྱབས་	to catch cold
ཆམས་པ་བསྐྱོན་	ཆམས་པ་སྐྱོན་	ཆམས་པ་བསྐྱོནད་	to catch cold (h)
གོ་	གོ་	གོ་	to hear, to understand
གསན་	གསན་	གསནད་	to hear (h)
ཧ་གོ་	ཧ་གོ་	ཧ་གོ་	to understand
མཁྱེན་	མཁྱེན་	མཁྱེནད་	to understand (h)
Unit 13			
ཚར་	ཚར་	ཚརད་	to finish
འགྲུབ་	འགྲུབ་	གྲུབ་	to finish (h)
གཉིད་འཁྱག་	གཉིད་འཁྱགས་	གཉིད་ཁྱགས་	to sleep
གཟིམ་འཁྱག་	གཟིམ་འཁྱགས་	གཟིམ་ཁྱགས་	to sleep (h)
བསྡོམ་	སྡོམ་	བསྡོམས་	to combine, to add
ཕྲེན་	འཕྲེན་	ཕྲེནད་	to reduce, to subtract
བགོ་	བགོ་	བགོས་	to divide, to share
Unit 14			
ཁྱེར་	འཁྱེར་	ཁྱེརད་	to bring, to carry
སྣམས་	སྣོམ་	བསྣམས་	to bring, to carry (h)
བླུག་	བླུག་	བླུགས་	to pour
བླུགས་གནང་	བླུགས་གནང་	བླུགས་གནང་	to pour (h)
བླང་/ལེན་	ལེན་	བླངས་	to take, to partake
བཞེས་	བཞེས་	བཞེས་	to take, to partake (h)

སྤྲོད་	སྤྲོད་	སྤྲོད་	to give
བསྐྱེར་	སྐྱེར་	བསྐྱེརད་	to give
གནང་	གནང་	གནང་	to give, to do (h)
འཇོལ་	འཇོལ་	འཇོལ་	to enter
འཇོལ་གནང་	འཇོལ་གནང་	འཇོལ་གནང་	to enter (h)
ཐུག་	ཐུག་	ཐུག་	to meet
མཇལ་ / མཇལ་གནང་	མཇལ་ / མཇལ་གནང་	མཇལད་ / མཇལ་གནང་	to meet (h)
སྐད་ཆ་འདྲི་	སྐད་ཆ་དྲི་	སྐད་ཆ་དྲིས་	to ask
བཀའ་འདྲི་གནང་	བཀའ་འདྲི་གནང་	བཀའ་འདྲི་གནང་	to ask (h)
ཞུ་	ཞུ་	ཞུས་	to request, to partake
ཞུས་གནང་	ཞུས་གནང་	ཞུས་གནང་	to request, to partake (h)
སྦྱོང་	སྦྱོང་	སྦྱངས་	to practice, to train, to learn
སྦྱངས་གནང་	སྦྱངས་གནང་	སྦྱངས་གནང་	to practice, to train, to learn (h)
འབུལ་	འབུལ་	ཕུལ་	to offer
ཕུལ་གནང་	ཕུལ་གནང་	ཕུལ་གནང་	to offer (h)

For drills changing tenses see Unit 12.47-12.49, 13.102-13.105, 14.52-14.60.

IMPERATIVE

In spoken Tibetan the imperative is constructed either by using the imperative form of the verbal root alone, as in བཞུགས། ("Sit down" h), or by adding an imperative ending—for instance, རོགས་གནང་ [literally, "help-do"]—to the verb root, as in ག་ལེར་ཕེབས་རོགས་གནང་ ("Please go well" h). The imperative has several different endings in order to indicate various levels of urgency and/or politeness. Below are various imperative forms of the verb ཕེབས་ ("to go" h). Most verbal roots can be substituted for ཕེབས་ in the following table:

༢ ཕེབས་རོགས་གནང་།   very mild imperative: "Please go." (h)

༣ ཕེབས་ཨ།   affectionate imperative said to a friend, child, or student: "Go." (h)

༣ ཕེབས་ན།   suggestive imperative: "If you went" or "What about going?" (h)

༤ ཕེབས་གོ།   gentle imperative: "Go." (h)

༥ ཕེབས་དང་།[1]   deferential insistent imperative: "Go." (h)

༦ ཕེབས་ཏོ།   self-inclusive imperative: "Let's go." (h)

༧ ཕེབས་ཤིག   insistent imperative: "Go." (h)

༨ ཕེབས།   "Go." (h)

The fourth line of the Unit 6 dialogue ང་གཉིས་མཉམ་དུ་ཕེབས་ཏོ། ("Let's go together") introduces the terminating particle ཏོ When used with a verb such as "to go", "to do", or "to eat", it conveys a mild imperative; it suggests "let's do" whatever the action in question is. For drills see Unit 12.74-12.108.

ADVERBS

INTENSIFIERS

In the Unit 10 dialogue Ḍa-shí and Tön-ḍup say that the restaurant is དངོས་གནས་ཡག་པོ་འདུག which means that it is really good. Ḍa-shí adds that it is *very* good: ཡག་པོ་ཞེ་དྲག་འདུག. The words དངོས་གནས་ and ཞེ་དྲག་ are intensifiers that amplify or intensify the meaning of the word they qualify, in this case ཡག་པོ. Others are ཞིད་པོ་ཅིག, དཔེ, and ཧ་ཅང. From among these, ཞེ་དྲག, ཞིད་པོ་ཅིག, and ཧ་ཅང are interchangeable, all meaning "very" although ཞིད་པོ་ ཅིག can indicate a further level of intensity such as "extremely". As was said above, དངོས་ གནས་ means "really"; དཔེ is an abbreviated form of དཔེ་མི་སྲིད་པ (literally, "that of which there is no example") and thus means "unparalleled" or "exceptionally". The intensifiers དངོས་གནས་, ཞེ་དྲག, and ཞིད་པོ་ཅིག *can* go either before or after the word they modify; however, དངོས་གནས་ usually precedes the word it modifies, whereas ཞེ་དྲག and ཞིད་པོ་ཅིག are used more or less equally before and after the words they modify. The intensifier དཔེ almost always precedes the word it modifies. The intensifier ཧ་ཅང always precedes the

---

[1] This ending is pronounced ḍa.

word it modifies. For drills see Unit 10.9-10.18, 13.70-13.71.

The intensifier རང་ qualifies adjectives only in negative expressions. In that situation རང་ plus the negative means "not really" or "not very". For instance, ཁོང་བདེ་པོ་རང་མི་འདུག means "She/ he is not really well" (h) and མང་པོ་རང་མི་འདུག means "There are not very many." For drills see Unit 10.20-10.24.

OTHER POSTPOSITIONAL PARTICLES

"TOO", "BUT", "EVEN"

The particle ཡང་ and its complementary particles ཀྱང་ and འང་ are used with both conjunctive meaning ("also") and disjunctive meaning ("but", "although") as well as with the sense of "even". The particle ཀྱང་ follows the suffixes ག་ ད་ བ་ ས་; the particle ཡང་ follows the suffixes ང་ ན་ མ་ ར་ ལ་ and sometimes words without a suffix; the particle འང་ follows the suffix འ་ as well as words without a suffix. In chart form:

Suffix	Ending
ག་ ད་ བ་ ས་	ཀྱང་
ང་ ན་ མ་ ར་ ལ་ or no suffix	ཡང་
འ་ or no suffix	འང་

The word ཡང་ ("too", "also") when spoken quickly is often pronounced as a long "é" "or "yé" as in the dialogue sentence ང་ཡང་ཁྲོམ་ལ་འགྲོ་གི་ཡིན། ("I too will go to the market"). However, if one is speaking slowly, the word should be pronounced "yang". For drills with the sense of "too" see Unit 6.5, 6.32, 6.40, 13.65.

In the dialogue in Unit 11, after the tea arrives, Dé-g̱yî̱ asks བོད་ཇ་ཞིམ་པོ་འདུག་གས། ("Is the Tibetan tea tasty?" h). Sö'-nam answers, "It is tasty but not hot" (ཞིམ་པོ་འདུག ཡིན་ནའང་ཚ་པོ་ མི་འདུག; literally, "It is tasty; even if it is [tasty], it is not hot," since ན་ means "if" and འང་ means "even".) This demonstrates how one says, "Yes, but..." using the construction ཡིན་ ནའང་ (pronounced "yînné>" and sometimes spelled ཡིན་ན་ཡང་ or even ཡིན་ནའི་). It is placed between the two qualities that are being set in contrast with one another; for instance, ཞིམ་ པོ་འདུག ཡིན་ནའང་ཚ་པོ་མི་འདུག ("It is tasty, but it is not hot"). To observe that something is good ཡག་པོ་ but expensive གོང་ཆེན་པོ་, one would say ཡག་པོ་འདུག ཡིན་ནའང་གོང་ཆེན་པོ་འདུག. For drills with the sense of "but" see Unit 11.6-11.8, 11.10-11.14

"EXCEPT"

In Unit 12 when Dor-jé asks Tom to make conversation, Tom insists ངས་དོངས་གནས་ལག་པོ་ ཤེས་ཀྱི་མེད། ("I don't know [Tibetan] really well"). He says that he knows some Tibetan but not much: ཏོག་ཙམ་ཏོག་ཙམ་མ་གཏོགས་ཤེས་ཀྱི་མེད།. His remark introduces a common idiomatic expression, "x" མ་གཏོགས་ ("y") མེད། which literally means, "except for x, not y". For instance, ཉུང་ཉུང་མ་གཏོགས་ཡོད་མ་རེད། means "Except for a few, there aren't any" or "There are only a few", and གསུམ་མ་གཏོགས་མི་འདུག or གསུམ་མ་གཏོགས་ཡོད་མ་རེད། means "Except for three, there aren't any" or "There are only three." For drills see Unit 12.72.-12.73.

The Unit 13 dialogue introduces the phrases ཆུ་ཚོད་གཅིག་མ་གཏོགས་འཛུག་གི་མ་རེད། ("It won't meet for more than one hour," or more literally "Except for one hour, [class] will not meet") and བཅུ་མ་གཏོགས་ཡོད་མ་རེད་པས། ("Are there no more than ten?" or more literally "Except for ten, are there none?"). Both sentences use མ་གཏོགས་ to express "except for". The term མ་ གཏོགས་ can also be translated as "only", in which case the above sentences would be rendered as "It meets for only one hour" and "Are there only ten?". As was explained just above, the term མ་གཏོགས་ is always used with a negative verb, as in the sentence ཇ་གྲང་མོ་མ་ གཏོགས་མི་འདུག ("There isn't anything except cold tea" or "There isn't anything but cold tea"). Sentences with མ་གཏོགས་ are quite common. For drills see Unit 13.62-12.63.

NUMBERS

For numbers in general see Unit 13.5-13.40.

TIME AND ORDINAL NUMBERS

In the Unit 13 dialogue when asked what time class will meet today, Bethany answers དེ་ རིང་ཆུ་ཚོད་བཅུ་པ་ལ་འཛུག་གི་རེད། ("Today [it] will meet at ten o'clock," or more literally, "Today [it] will meet at the tenth hour"). In Tibetan, hours are calculated with ordinal numbers: the first hour, the second hour, the third hour, and so on. Ordinal numbers are made by adding the syllable པ་ to the cardinal number. For instance, བཅུ་པ་ means "the tenth", as we have seen in this dialogue. There is one exception: གཅིག་ means "one", but གཅིག་པ་ does not mean "the first"; rather, it means "the same", as in དེ་གཉིས་གཅིག་པ་རེད་ ("Those two are the same"). "The first" is དང་པོ་. That is the only exception, for བཅུ་གཅིག་པ་ is the ordinal equivalent of བཅུ་གཅིག་, and ཉི་ཤུ་རྩ་གཅིག་པ་ is the ordinal equivalent of ཉི་ཤུ་རྩ་གཅིག་, and so on. For drills converting cardinal to ordinal numbers see Unit 13.41-13.44.

HOURS

The hours of the day are formed by combining ཆུ་ཚོད་ ("hour") with an ordinal number such as གཉིས་པ་ ("second"), making ཆུ་ཚོད་གཉིས་པ་ ("two o'clock"; literally, "second hour"). Notice that "one o'clock" is ཆུ་ཚོད་དང་པོ་, but "eleven o'clock" is ཆུ་ཚོད་བཅུ་གཅིག་པ་. For drills see Unit 13.45-13.47.

TELLING TIME

As with other languages, in ordinary conversation in Tibetan time is told in terms of two twelve-hour cycles. If there is some question about whether one means, for instance, six o'clock in the morning or six o'clock in the evening, one can use ཞོགས་ཀས་ ("morning") to indicate the hours before noon and དགོང་དག་ ("evening") to indicate the hours after noon. Thus, ཞོགས་ཀས་ཆུ་ཚོད་དྲུག་པ་ means "six o'clock in the morning", and དགོང་དག་ཆུ་ཚོད་དྲུག་པ་ means "six o'clock in the evening".

To tell the time, one states the hour and then the number of minutes. Hours alone, like two o'clock, are measured with ordinal numbers, but when combined with minutes after the hour, both hour and minutes are counted with cardinal numbers. For instance, to say, "Now it is 2:10", one says, ད་ལྟ་ཆུ་ཚོད་གཉིས་དང་སྐར་མ་བཅུ་རེད། The word ད་ལྟ་ means "now", and སྐར་མ་ means "minute".

The half-hour is stated with the cardinal number plus the words དང་ཕྱེད་ཀ ("and a half"), as in ཆུ་ཚོད་གཉིས་དང་ཕྱེད་ཀ ("two-thirty").

As in English, the second half of an hour can be counted either by the number of minutes that have elapsed since the previous hour or by the number of minutes remaining until the next hour. For instance, to say "2:45", one could say either ཆུ་ཚོད་གཉིས་དང་སྐར་མ་བཞི་བཅུ་ཞེ་ལྔ་ or ཆུ་ཚོད་གསུམ་པ་ཉེན་པ་ལ་སྐར་མ་བཅོ་ལྔ་. In this context, ཉེན་པ་ means "reaching"; the phrase literally means "fifteen minutes til reaching three o'clock". Notice that the དང་ form uses a cardinal number while the ཉེན་པ་ form uses an ordinal number. For drills see Unit 13.48-13.55.

HOW MANY HOURS FROM HERE TO THERE?

The verb འགོར་ ("to take time") is used in asking how much time something will take. For instance, བོད་ནས་སོག་ཡུལ་ལ་ཆུ་ཚོད་ག་ཚོད་འགོར་གྱི་རེད། means "How many hours will it take [to go] from Tibet to Mongolia?" For a drill see Unit 13.57.

MATHEMATICAL OPERATIONS: ཨང་རྩིས་

1. ADDITION: སྣོམ་རྩིས་

To add two numbers such as གཅིག་ and བཞི་ one says གཅིག་དང་བཞི་བསྡོམས་ན་ལྔ་རེད། (literally, "If one and four are combined, [the total] is five" or, in other words, "One plus four is five"). The word བསྡོམས་ means "combine". Notice that before ན་ ("if" or "when") the past tense is used. Other ways of doing addition are གཅིག་དང་བཞི་ཕྱིས་ན་ལྔ་རེད། and གཅིག་སྟེང་ལ་བཞི་ རྒྱབ་ན་ལྔ་རེད།. For a drill see Unit 13.37.

2. SUBTRACTION: འཐེན་རྩིས་

To subtract one number from another, such as བཞི་ ("four") from དྲུག་ ("six"), one says དྲུག་ ནས་བཞི་འཐེན་ན་གཉིས་རེད། (Literally, "If four is subtracted from six, [the remainder] is two" or, in other words, "Six minus four is two"). For a drill see Unit 13.38.

3. MULTIPLICATION: སྒྱུར་རྩིས་

To multiply two numbers such as གཉིས་ and བཞི་ one says གཉིས་བཞི་ལ་བརྒྱད་རེད། (literally, "In four twos are twenty-five" or, in other words, "Two times four is eight"). For a drill see Unit 13.39.

4. DIVISION: བགོས་རྩིས་

To divide one number by another, such as བཞི་ ("four") by གཉིས་ ("two"), one says བཞི་ གཉིས་ལ་བགོས་ན་གཉིས་རེད། (literally, "If four is divided in two, [the quotient] is two" or, in other words, "Four divided by two is two"). For a drill see Unit 13.40.

ETIQUETTE

GREETINGS

The most common way to start a conversation in Tibetan with an acquaintance you meet on the street is ག་པར་ཕེབས་ཀ། ("Where are you going?"), not "Hello" or "How are you?" as in English. From much contact with Westerners, some Tibetans have picked up the custom of using the phrase བཀྲ་ཤིས་བདེ་ལེགས། (literally, "good luck") as a greeting, particularly to foreigners. However, the question ག་པར་ཕེབས་ཀ། ("Where are you going?" h) is still what Tibetans commonly say to acquaintances when they meet on the street. This is used only when meeting someone you already know, and not when initiating conversations with a stranger.

The Unit 5 dialogue presents a standard exchange of greetings that Tibetans use when one acquaintance arrives at the home or town of another:

སྐུ་གཟུགས་བདེ་པོ་ཡིན་པས།

ང་བདེ་པོ་ཡིན། ཁྱེད་རང་སྐུ་གཟུགས་བདེ་པོ་ཡིན་པས།

བདེ་པོ་ཡིན།

It is idiomatic, and a literal translation does not express the full meaning and flavor of the exchange. For now, just memorize it, and gradually develop a sense of the exchange. Note that there are several possible responses to the question སྐུ་གཟུགས་བདེ་པོ་ཡིན་པས། ("Are you well?" h). In Unit 4, the responses given are ང་བདེ་པོ་ཡིན། ("I am well"), simply ལགས་ཡིན། (literally, "Yes, [I] am"), and ལགས་བདེ་པོ་ཡིན། (literally, "Yes, [I] am well"). The response given is influenced by factors such as the degree of formality of the situation.

"THANK YOU"

The Unit 5 dialogue introduces the Tibetan word for "thank you" ཐུགས་རྗེ་ཆེ་. It is important to keep in mind that Tibetans use ཐུགས་རྗེ་ཆེ་ far less frequently than Americans, for instance, use "thank you". Three specific occasions where "thank you" is used in English but ཐུགས་རྗེ་ཆེ་ is not used in Tibetan are:

1   In response to the question ཁྱེད་རང་སྐུ་གཟུགས་བདེ་པོ་ཡིན་པས། ("Are you well?"). In English, "I am fine, thank you," is a polite response whereas in Tibetan it would be odd to add ཐུགས་རྗེ་ཆེ་ to one's answer.

2   When refusing something that has been offered to you. In English, "No, thank you" is a polite negative response. In Tibetan, one merely says ལགས་མིན། ("No"). The particle ལགས་ here conveys appropriate politeness.

3   Upon receiving a compliment, English speakers say, "Thank you," whereas Tibetan speakers remain silent. For Tibetans, to say ཐུགས་རྗེ་ཆེ་ after a compliment would suggest that the compliment was insincere.

" 'TIL WE MEET AGAIN"

In concluding their conversation in Unit 14, Tom and Ḏöl-ma say ཡང་སྐྱར་མཇལ་ཡོང་ to one another. ཡང་ means "again", སྐྱར་ means "repeat", མཇལ་ means "to meet", and ཡོང་ means "to come" and is a future indicator. Thus ཡང་སྐྱར་མཇལ་ཡོང་ means "We'll meet again" or "See you again." Tibetans also frequently say མགྱོགས་པོ་མཇལ་ཡོང་, which means "We'll meet soon" or "See you soon."

Tape Errata

The occasional mis-readings that occurred in the process of recording the twenty-six hours of practice material are listed in this section.

Drill 4.13.1: Tape omits ཚེ་རིང་ in middle column.

Drill 4.20.7: Tape misreads ཁོང་བློ་བཟང་ལགས་རེད་པས། for བློ་བཟང་ལགས་ཡིན་པས།.

Drill 4.23.7: Tape reverses left and right columns.

Drill 4.23.9: Tape omits misreads ཁོང་བོད་པ་རེད། for ཁོང་བོད་པ་རེད་པས།.

Drill 5.8.14: Tape

Drill 5.8.18: Tape misreads ང་ཨུ་རུ་སུ་མིན། for ཨུ་རུ་སུ་མིན།.

Drill 6.5.3: Tape misreads ཁོང་ཚོ་ཡང་ཁྲིམ་ལ་ཕེབས་ཀྱི་རེད། for ཁོང་ཡང་ཁྲིམ་ལ་ཕེབས་ཀྱི་རེད།.

Drill 6.6.3: Tape misreads ང་གཉིས་མཉམ་དུ་འགྲོ་ཧོ། for ང་རང་ཚོ་མཉམ་དུ་འགྲོ་ཧོ།.

Drill 6.6.5: Tape misreads ང་གཉིས་མཉམ་དུ་མཆོད་ཧོ། for ང་རང་ཚོ་མཉམ་དུ་མཆོད་ཧོ།.

Drill 6.7.9: Tape misreads ཁོང་ཚོ་ཕེབས་ཀྱི་རེད་པས། for ཁོང་ཚོ་ཕེབས་ཀྱི་རེད།.

Drill 6.14.1: Tape misreads ཁོང་སློན་ཁང་ལ་ཕེབས་ཀྱི་རེད། for ཁོང་ཚོ་སློན་ཁང་ལ་ཕེབས་ཀྱི་རེད།.

Drill 6.15.8: Tape misreads ཐུབ་བསྟན་ for ཐུབ་བསྟན་ལགས་.

Drill 6.58.2: Tape misreads ང་བོད་ལ་འགྲོ་གི་ཡིན། for ང་ཚོ་བོད་ལ་འགྲོ་གི་ཡིན།.

Drill 6.58.3: Tape misreads མོ་ནང་ལ་འགྲོ་གི་རེད། for ཁོ་ནང་ལ་འགྲོ་གི་རེད།.

Drill 7.52.4-7.52.8: Tape misreads ག་པར་འདུག་གས། for ག་པར་འདུག།.

Drill 7.30.1 and 7.30.5: Tape reads ག་པར་ཕེབས་མཁན་ཡིན་པ། for ག་པར་ཕེབས་མཁན་ཡིན།; both versions are suitable.

Drill 8.11.2: Tape misreads ཁྱེད་རང་བོད་ལ་ཕེབས་ཀྱི་ཡིན་པས། for ཁྱེད་རང་ཚོ་བོད་ལ་ཕེབས་ཀྱི་ཡིན་པས།.

Drill 8.14.2: Tape misreads ཁྱེད་རང་ཀི་ལ་མཆོད་གས། for ཁྱེད་རང་ཀི་ལ་གཟིགས་གས།.

Drill 8.21.1: Tape misreads པད་མ་ལགས་ནང་ལ་ཕེབས་ཀྱི་རེད་པས། for པད་མ་ལགས་གཉིམ་ཁང་ལ་ཕེབས་ཀྱི་རེད།.

Drill 8.23.3: Tape misreads ང་ཚོ་སློན་ཁང་ལ་འགྲོ་མཁན་རེད། for ང་ཚོ་སློན་ཁང་ལ་འགྲོ་མཁན་ཡིན།.

Drill 8.24.5 and 8.24.9: Tape reads ག་པར་ཕེབས་མཁན་ཡིན་པ། for ག་པར་ཕེབས་མཁན་ཡིན།; both versions are suitable.

Drill 8.25.2: Tape misreads སྒྲོལ་མ་ལགས་ཡིན་པས། for སྒྲོལ་མ་ལགས་མིན་པས།.

Drill 9.5.1: Tape misreads དངུལ་ཁང་ཆེན་པོ་ཅིག་ག་པར་འདུག་གས། for དངུལ་ཁང་ཆེན་པོ་ཅིག་ག་པར་འདུག།.

Drill 9.6.2: Middle and right columns of tape misread སྡུག་ཆག་ for སྡུག་ཆག་དེ་.

Drill 9.14.3: Tape misreads “some dwellings” for “some inns”.

Drill 9.22.1, 9.22.2, 9.22.4, 9.22.5: Left column of tape misreads རེད་པས། for རེད།.

Drill 9.23.6: Tape misreads དེ་སྨན་ཁང་རྙིང་པ་རེད། for དེ་སྨན་ཁང་རྙིང་པ་ཅིག་རེད།.

Drill 9.23.8: Tape misreads དེ་ཆང་ཁང་ཡག་པོ་ཡོད་རེད། for དེ་ཆང་ཁང་ཡག་པོ་ཅིག་རེད།.

Drill 9.26.1: Tape misreads དེ་རིང་ལྷ་སར་འགྲོ་གི་ཡིན། for དེ་རིང་འགྲོ་གི་ཡིན།.

Drill 9.36.3 second time: Tape misreads བཞིས་བག་ for བཞིས་འབྲས་.

Drill 9.52: Tape misreads “Drill 9.53” for “Drill 9.52”.

Drill 10.5.7: Tape misreads ཁོང་ལ་དངུལ་མང་པོ་ for ཁོང་ལ་ཕྱུག་དངུལ་མང་པོ་ in both columns.

Drill 10.6.7: Tape misreads ཁོང་ལ་དངུལ་མང་པོ་ for ཁོང་ལ་ཕྱུག་དངུལ་མང་པོ་ in both columns.

Drill 10.7.2: Tape reads དགོན་པ་ལ་གྲང་མོ་ for དགོན་པའི་ནང་ལ་གྲང་མོ་; both versions are acceptable although the latter is more proper.

Drill 10.8.1: Tape misreads རྒྱ་ནག་ལ་དགོན་པ་ཡོད་མ་རེད། for རྒྱ་ནག་ལ་དགོན་པ་ཡོད་མ་རེད་པས།.

Drill 10.8.12: Tape misreads ཁོང་ལ་དངུལ་མང་པོ་ for ཁོང་ལ་ཕྱུག་དངུལ་མང་པོ་ in both columns.

Drill 10.12.4: Tape misreads མི་དེ་སྡུག་ཆག་འདུག། for མི་དེ་དཔེ་སྡུག་ཆག་འདུག།.

Drill 10.19.2: Tape misreads ང་ཚོ་དགོན་པ་ལ་འགྲོ་གི་རེད། for ང་ཚོ་དགོན་པ་ལ་ཕེབས་ཀྱི་རེད།.

Drill 10.20.1: Tape misreads ང་རང་ཕྱུག་པོ་རང་མིན། for ང་ཕྱུག་པོ་རང་མིན།.

Drill 10.38.5: Tape omits the middle column ཆབ་མང་ར་མོ་.

Drill 10.38.6: Tape omits the middle column བཞིས་སོག་.

Drill 10.46.: Middle and right columns misread ཙམ་པ་ for ཐུ་པ་.

Drill 10.46.6: Middle column of tape misreads ཐུག་པ་བཛོ་ for ཐུག་པ་བཟོ་.

Drill 11.9: Drill title should read: Responding “No, it isn’tṇ, butṇ” to “ṇisn’tṇ, is it?” (མི་འདུག་ག་).

Drill 11.9.1: Tape misreads གསོལ་ཇ་འདི་གོང་ཁི་པོ་མི་འདུག་ག། for གསོལ་ཇ་འདི་གོང་ཆེན་པོ་མི་འདུག་ག།.

Drill 11.10: Drill title should read: Responding “No, it isn’tṇ, butṇ” to “ṇisn’tṇ, is it?” (མི་འདུག་ག་).

Drill 11.11: Drill title should read: Responding “No, there is no A, but there is B” to ཡོད་རེད་པས་.

Drill 11.11.3: Tape misreads ཁྲོམ་ལ་འབྲས་ཡོད་མ་རེད་པས། for ཁྲོམ་ལ་འབྲས་ཡོད་རེད་པས།.

Drill 11.12.1: Tape misreads ཨེན་ནཝང་ཟ་ཁང་མང་པོ་ཡོད་རེད། for ཨེན་ནཝང་ཟ་ཁང་ཨག་པོ་ཡོད་རེད།.

Drill 11.23: Drill number and title should read: DRILL 11.23: Responding to "How isṇ?" questions with འདུག, negative, with the subject.

Drill 11.34.13: Tape misreads གཟའ་སྟེན་པར་བྱེད་ཀྱི་རེད། for གཟའ་སྟེན་པར་བྱེད་ཀྱི་ཨིན།.

Drill 12.5.1: Tape reads ང་མཚོ་འགྲམ་ལ་འགྲོ་གི་ཡོད། for ང་མཚོ་ལ་འགྲོ་གི་ཡོད།; both versions are suitable. The word འགྲམ means "shore" or "bank".

Drill 12.6.5: Tape misreads ལྷ་ཁང་ for ལྷ་ཁང་གི་འགྲིས་ ("next to the temple"). There usually are not guest quarters in Tibetan temples.

Drill 12.18.5: Left column of tape misreads ལགས་ཁོང་ལ་ཞལ་ལག་དགོས་གནང་གི་ཡོད་རེད་པས། for ལགས་ཁོང་ལ་ཞལ་ལག་དགོས་གནང་གི་ཡོད་རེད།.

Drill 12.20.1: Tape misreads ཁོང་གིས་གཟིམ་ཁང་ལ་ཕྱག་ལས་གནང་གི་ཡོད་རེད། for ཁོང་གིས་གཟིམ་ཁང་ལ་ཕྱག་ལས་གནང་གི་ཡོད་རེད་པས།.

Drill 12.21.1: Tape misreads ང་གཞིས་ཀ་རྩེ་ལ་འགྲོ་གི་རེད། for ང་གཞིས་ཀ་རྩེ་ལ་འགྲོ་གི་ཡོད་རེད། .

Drill 12.22.1: Tape misreads ང་ཚོ་གནས་ཚང་ལ་བསྡད་ཀྱི་ཡོད། for ང་ཚོ་གནས་ཚང་ལ་བསྡད་ཀྱི་ཡོད་རེད། .

Drill 12.36.1-4: Right column of tape misreads ཁྱེད་ཚོས་ for ཁྱེད་རང་ཚོས་.

Drill 12.49.10 & 11: Tape reads ཕྱག་བྲིས་གནང་གི་ཡོད་རེད། for ཕྱག་བྲིས་བྲིས་གནང་གི་ཡོད་རེད།; both versions are suitable.

Drill 12.55.3: Tape misreads ཁོང་གིས་ཨིན་ཇིའི་སྐད་ཡག་པོ་མཁྱེན་གྱི་འདུག for ཁོང་ཨིན་ཇིའི་སྐད་ཡག་པོ་མཁྱེན་གྱི་འདུག.

Drill 12.58.7: Tape misreads མོས་བུ་ལ་ཁ་པར་བཏང་གི་འདུག for མོས་བུ་མོ་ལ་ཁ་པར་བཏང་གི་འདུག.

Drill 12.66.6: Tape misreads མོག་མོག་རྔངས་བཙོས་སྐྱོན་གྱི་ཡོད་རེད། for བཞེས་མོག་རྔངས་བཙོས་སྐྱོན་གྱི་ཡོད་རེད།.

Drill 12.67.9: Tape misreads ཕྱག་དེབ་འདི་ཁོ་ཚོའི་རེད། for དེབ་འདི་ཁོ་ཚོའི་རེད།.

Drill 12.77.9: Tape reads ཕྱག་བྲིས་མ་གནང་རོགས་གནང་། for ཕྱག་བྲིས་བྲིས་མ་གནང་རོགས་གནང་།; both versions are suitable.

Drill 12.81.9: Tape reads ཕྱག་བྲིས་མ་གནང་ཨ། for ཕྱག་བྲིས་བྲིས་མ་གནང་ཨ།; both versions are suitable.

Drill 12.85.9: Tape reads ཕྱག་བྲིས་མ་གནང་ན། for ཕྱག་བྲིས་བྲིས་མ་གནང་ན།; both versions are suitable.

Drill 12.92.9: Tape reads ཕྱག་བྲིས་བྲིས་མ་གནང་དང་། for ཕྱག་བྲིས་བྲིས་མ་གནང་དང་།; both versions are suitable.

Drill 12.99.9: Tape reads ཕྱུག་བྲིས་གནང་ཤིག། for ཕྱུག་ཕྲིས་བྲིས་གནང་ཤིག།; both versions are suitable.

Drill 12.99.9: Tape reads ཕྱུག་བྲིས་མ་གནང་ཤིག། for ཕྱུག་བྲིས་བྲིས་མ་གནང་ཤིག།; both versions are suitable.

Drill 12.103.9: Tape reads ཕྱུག་བྲིས་མ་གནང་། for ཕྱུག་བྲིས་བྲིས་མ་གནང་།; both versions are suitable.

Drill 13.41.3: Tape misreads གསུམ་ for གསུམ་པ་.

Drill 13.62.1: Tape misreads ང་གྲུང་མོ་མ་གཏོགས་མེ་འདུག། for ང་མཛར་མོ་མ་གཏོགས་མེ་འདུག།.

Drill 13.64.3: Middle and right columns of tape misread ཚེམ་པ་ for ཕྱུག་པ་.

Drill 13.66.5: Middle and right columns of tape misread ལྷ་ཁང་ for མགྲོན་ཁང་.

Drill 13.78.2: Middle column of tape misreads ཁོང་གི་ for ཁྱེད་རང་གི་.

Drill 13.79.1: Tape misreads ཁོང་ཚོ་ཨ་མེ་རི་ཀའི་དགོན་པ་ལ་བཞུགས་ཀྱི་ཡོད་མ་རེད་པས་ for ཁོང་ཚོ་ཨ་རིའི་དགོན་པ་ལ་བཞུགས་ཀྱི་ཡོད་མ་རེད་པས་.

Drill 13.83.12: Tape misreads ང་དྲན་གྱི་མེ་འདུག for ང་དྲན་གྱི་ཡོད་མ་རེད།.

Drill 13.83.13: Tape misreads ང་འདིའི་འདྲས་བསམ་གྱི་མེ་འདུག for ང་འདིའི་འདྲས་བསམ་གྱི་ཡོད་མ་རེད།.

Drill 13.84.1: Middle column of tape omits ཁྱེད་རང་.

Drill 13.84.3: Tape misreads ལགས་མཐུན་གྱི་འདུག ངག་དབང་ལགས་དང་མཐུན་གྱི་འདུག for ལགས་མཐུན་གནང་གི་འདུག ངག་དབང་ལགས་དང་མཐུན་གནང་གི་འདུག.

Drill 13.84.4: Tape misreads ངག་དབང་ལགས་དང་མཐུན་གྱི་མེ་འདུག for ངག་དབང་ལགས་དང་མཐུན་གནང་གི་མེ་འདུག.

Drill 13.84.5: Middle column of tape omits ཁྱེད་རང་. Also, right column reads ལགས་འཁྱག་གནང་གི་འདུག ཁྱེད་རང་འཁྱག་གནང་གི་འདུག for ལགས་སྐུ་བསིལ་གྱི་འདུག ཁྱེད་རང་སྐུ་བསིལ་གྱི་འདུག; both versions are suitable.

Drill 13.84.6: Middle column of tape omits ཁྱེད་རང་.

Drill 13.101.1: Tape misreads བོས་དགོན་པ་ལ་ལས་ཀ་ཚར་གྱི་ཡོད་མ་རེད། for བོས་དགོན་པ་ལ་ལས་ཀ་ཚར་གྱི་ཡོད་མ་རེད་པས།.

Drill 13.101.2: Tape misreads ཁྱེད་རང་གིས་དགོན་པ་ལ་ལས་ཀ་ཚར་གྱི་མེ་འདུག for ཁྱེད་རང་གིས་དགོན་པ་ལ་ལས་ཀ་ཚར་གྱི་མེ་འདུག་གས།.

Drill 13.103.12: Tape misreads ཁོང་གིས་སྐལ་བཟང་ལགས་མཇལ་གྱི་རེད། for ཁོང་གིས་སྐལ་བཟང་ལགས་མཇལ་གནང་གི་རེད།.

Drill 14.6.1, 14.6.2, 14.6.5: Tape reads ཟེར་གྱི་ཡོད། for ཟེར་གྱི་ཡོད་རེད།; both versions are suitable.

Drill 14.8.1: Tape misreads ཁོའི་མིང་ལ་པད་མ་དང་ཁོའི་མིང་བདེ་སྐྱིད་རེད། for ཁོའི་མིང་པད་མ་དང་

ཕོའི་མེང་བདེ་སྐྱིད་རེད།.

Drill 14.8.2: Tape misreads ཁོའི་མེང་ལ་ཚེ་རིང་རེད། for ཁོའི་མེང་ཚེ་རིང་རེད།.

Drill 14.8.4: Tape misreads ཁོའི་མེང་ལ་རྒྱ་མཚོ་དང་ཁོའི་མེང་བསོད་ནམས་རེད། for ཁོའི་མེང་རྒྱ་མཚོ་དང་ཁོའི་མེང་བསོད་ནམས་རེད།.

Drill 14.10.1: Tape misreads ངས་ཁོང་ལ་དངུལ་ཏོག་ཙམ་ཕུལ་པ་ཡིན། for ངས་ཁོང་ལ་ཕྱུག་དངུལ་ཏོག་ཙམ་ཕུལ་པ་ཡིན།.

Drill 14.10.5: Middle column of tape misreads གསོལ་ཇ་མང་ར་མོ་ for ཇ་མང་ར་མོ་.

Drill 14.14.1: Tape misreads ངས་ཁོང་ལ་དངུལ་མ་ཕུལ། for ངས་ཁོང་ལ་ཕྱུག་དངུལ་མ་ཕུལ།.

Drill 14.14.2: Tape misreads ངས་ཁོང་ལ་མོག་མོག་མང་པོ་མ་ཕུལ། for ངས་ཁོང་ལ་བཞེས་མོག་མང་པོ་མ་ཕུལ།.

Drill 14.14.3: Tape misreads ངས་ཁོང་ལ་ཁ་ལག་ཡག་པོ་མ་ཕུལ། for ངས་ཁོང་ལ་ཞལ་ལག་ཡག་པོ་མ་ཕུལ།.

Drill 14.27.1: Tape reads ཁོང་གིས་དགེ་རྒན་ལགས་ལ་ཕྱག་དངུལ་ཕུལ་གནང་སོང་། for ཁོང་གིས་རྒན་ལགས་ལ་ཕྱག་དངུལ་ཕུལ་གནང་སོང་།; both versions are suitable

Drill 14.30.4: Tape misreads ལགས་མ་ཉལ་པ་རེད། མདངས་དགོང་མ་ཉལ་པ་རེད། for ལགས་ཡག་པོ་མ་ཉལ་པ་རེད། མདངས་དགོང་ཡག་པོ་མ་ཉལ་པ་རེད།.

Drill 14.44.3: Tape misreads ཁྱེད་རང་ཚོས་བོད་ལ་ཁ་པར་བཏང་གནང་སོང་། for ཁྱེད་རང་ཚོས་བོད་ལ་ཞལ་པར་བཏང་གནང་སོང་།.

Drill 14.45.1: Tape misreads ཁྱེད་རང་གིས་གསོལ་ཇ་མ་བཞེས་པ་རེད། for ཁྱེད་རང་གིས་ཇ་མ་བཞེས་པ་རེད།.

Drill 14.49: Drill title should read: Alternative past negative interrogative, first person, auxiliary verb and pronoun substitution

Drill 14.50: Drill title should read: Alternative past negative interrogative, third person, auxiliary verb and pronoun substitution

Drill 14.50.1: Tape misreads ཁོང་གིས་བླ་མ་དེ་ལ་ཁ་བཏགས་ཕུལ་གནང་སོང་ངས། for ཁོང་གིས་བླ་མ་དེ་ལ་ཁ་བཏགས་ཕུལ་གནང་མ་སོང་ངས།.

Drill 14.50.2: Tape misreads ཁོང་ཚོས་བླ་མ་དེ་ལ་ཁ་བཏགས་བསྣམས་སོང་ངས། for ཁོང་ཚོས་བླ་མ་དེ་ལ་ཁ་བཏགས་བསྣམས་མ་སོང་ངས།.

Drill 14.50.3: Tape misreads ཁོང་ཚོ་མདངས་དགོང་དགོན་པ་ལ་ཕེབས་སོང་ངས། for ཁོང་ཚོ་མདངས་དགོང་དགོན་པ་ལ་ཕེབས་མ་སོང་ངས།.

Drill 14.51: Drill title should read: Alternative past negative interrogative, first person, auxiliary verb and object substitution

Drill 14.51.3: Tape misreads ང་ཚོས་ཁོང་མཇལ་སོང་ངས། for ང་ཚོས་ཁོང་མཇལ་མ་སོང་ངས།.

Drill 14.53.32: Tape misreads ཁོང་ལུག་ཤ་མཆོད་སོང་། for ཁོང་ལུག་ཤ་མཆོད་སོང་ངས།.

Drill 14.54.9: Tape misreads ཁོ་དཔེ་མཛོད་ཁང་ལ་འགྲོ་གི་འདུག for ཁོ་ཚོ་དཔེ་མཛོད་ཁང་ལ་འགྲོ་གི་ འདུག.

Drill 15.6.6: Tape misreads རྙིང་པོ་རེད། for རྙིང་པོ་འདུག.

Drill 15.20.3: Tape misreads ཁོ་ཚོ་ཕྱུག་པོ་མ་རེད། for ང་ཚོ་ཕྱུག་པོ་མ་རེད།.

Drill 15.29.1: Tape misreads བོད་ཇ་འདི་གོང་ཆེན་པོ་མེ་འདུག་གས། for བོད་ཇ་འདི་གོང་ཁི་པོ་མེ་འདུག་ གས།.

Drill 15.39.3: Tape reads ངས་སྒུག་ཁང་མཐོང་གི་འདུག for ང་སྒུག་ཁང་མཐོང་གི་འདུག; both ver-sions are suitable.

Drill 15.42.13: Middle column of tape omits སློབ་སྦྱོང་གནང་.

Drill 15.42.13: Tape misreads ཁྱེད་རང་ཚོས་གཉིམ་ཁང་ལ་ཕྱག་བྲིས་སློབ་སྦྱོང་གནང་གི་ཡོད་པས། for ཁྱེད་རང་ཚོས་གཉིམ་ཁང་ལ་སློབ་སྦྱོང་གནང་གི་ཡོད་པས།.

Drill 15.43.1: Tape misreads ཁྱེད་རང་ཁ་པར་བཏང་གནང་གི་ཡོད་པས། for ཁྱེད་རང་ཞལ་པར་བཏང་ གནང་གི་ཡོད་པས།.

Drill 15.44.3: Middle column of tape misreads ཞལ་ལག་བཟོ་ for ཁ་ལག་བཟོ་.

Drill 15.62.1: Tape misreads ཁོས་དགོན་པ་ལ་ལས་ཀ་ཆར་གྱི་ཡོད་མ་རེད། for ཁོས་དགོན་པ་ལ་ལས་ཀ་ ཆར་གྱི་ཡོད་མ་རེད་པས།.

Drill 15.69.4: Tape misreads མོ་རང་ཚོས་ལས་ཀ་ལས་སླ་པོ་དེ་བྱས་མ་སོང་ངས། for མོ་རང་ཚོས་ལས་ ཀ་ལས་སླ་པོ་དེ་བྱས་སོང་ངས།.

Drill 15.74.9: Tape misreads སྐལ་བཟང་ལ་ཁ་པར་གཏང་ངས། for སྐལ་བཟང་ལ་ཁ་པར་གཏང་གས།.

Drill 15.79.34: Tape misreads རྒྱ་ཚོད་དྲུག་དང་ཕྱེད་ཀ་ལ་ཟ་གི་ཨིན། for རྒྱ་ཚོད་དྲུག་དང་ཕྱེད་ཀ་ལ་ཟ་ གི་ཡོད།.

Drill 15.79.42: Tape reads ཕྱག་ལས་ག་རེ་གནང་གི་ཡོད། for ཕྱག་ལས་ག་རེ་གནང་གི་ཡོད་རེད།; both versions are suitable.